SUPERBIKE

THE OFFICIAL BOOK 2011/2012

Claudio and Fabrizio Porrozzi

Giorgio NADA Editore

SUMMARY

That's Superbike	04
WSBK Champion	16
WSBK Riders	24
WSBK Races	36
Teams	116
Bikes 2011	130
Tyres	162
WSS Championship	168
STK 1000 Championship	184
STK 600 Championship	196
Standings	204
Champions	206

Giorgio Nada Editore Srl

Editorial Coordination
Leonardo Acerbi

Created by
Claudio Porrozzi
Gordon Ritchie (Technology)

Photo Editor
Fabrizio Porrozzi

Art director
Cinzia Giuriolo

Editing
Giorgio Nada Editore

Photographs
Fabrizio Porrozzi
Alessandro Piredda
Italo Santolini (Supersport)
Picture page 47 (Berger) by Mauro Mazzero (Team Supersonic)

© 2011 Giorgio Nada Editore, Vimodrone (Milano) - Italy

ALL RIGHTS RESERVED

All rights reserved. Apart from any fair dealing for the purpose of private study, research, criticism or review, no part of this publication may be reproduced, stored in a retrieval system, or transmitted, by any means, electronic, electrical, chemical, mechanical, optical photocopying, recording or otherwise, without prior written permission. All enquiries should be addressed to the publisher:

Giorgio Nada Editore
Via Claudio Treves, 15/17
I – 20090 VIMODRONE - MI
Tel. +39 02 27301126
Fax +39 02 27301454
E-mail: info@giorgionadaeditore.it
http://www.giorgionadaeditore.it

The catalogue of Giorgio Nada Editore publications is available on request at the above address.

Distributed by:
Giunti Editore Spa
via Bolognese 165
I – 50139 FIRENZE
www.giunti.it

Superbike 2011-2012. The Official Book
ISBN.978-88-7911-527-8

Here we are at the end of the 24th season of the FIM Superbike World Championship. The 2011 season gave us fantastic racing and – as in 2010 - a wonderful finish. It was the turn of a well-known, experienced rider to take the FIM World Superbike title, a rider with a long career in motorcycle sport and the first Spaniard to be crowned in this championship: Carlos Checa. He achieved a magnificent season, winning 15 races out of 26 and failing to score in only one race. This year has also been a success for the Italian manufacturer Ducati. Checa's success – and good results by other riders as well – is also due to a top-level motorcycle and structure and very efficient factory support to the teams. This shows the high level of competition in this Championship where so many manufacturers are involved. As during recent years, the Championship for production series motorcycles remains very attractive. Even if the motorcycle market is declining for economic reasons, this does not affect the success of racing.

The FIM Supersport Championship season has also been very exciting, with great racing in all rounds, and the title being clinched by British rider Chaz Davies on a Yamaha. Ducati also fought back in the FIM Superstock 1000 Cup, dominating the season and winning the title with Italian rider Davide Giugliano. This Cup has given us a great show, providing us with great competition and a very high level in riding and skill.

I would first like to congratulate the 2011 FIM Champions: Carlos Checa, Chaz Davies and Davide Giugliano – and then all the persons involved in the FIM Superbike & Supersport World Championships and FIM Superstock 1000 Cup; our partner Infront Motor Sports; the National Federations; the organisers, and all the riders and teams, the media and, of course, the spectators who are an essential part of our sport.

Vito Ippolito
President FIM

Throughout this season's 24th edition, the FIM Superbike World Championship continued to provide some of the most exciting racing on the planet. In 2011 the world's leading production-based racing series again lived up to its reputation for close, uncertain action on the track as well as an extraordinarily high technical level of modern-day superbike machinery in the pit and paddock.

Despite the general economic situation, Infront Motor Sports worked hard throughout the year to guarantee a quality field in World Superbike, World Supersport and the two thriving Superstock categories, and we were rewarded with the presence of eight manufacturers in the three classes, a vast range of professional, private teams and a multi-national line-up of participants that has no equal in international bike racing.

The eventual victory of Carlos Checa was also just reward for a rider who has been an integral part of the racing scene for many a year, but who reached a peak of competitive maturity with the Althea Racing team in 2011.

Next season sees World Superbike heading into its 25th year, and to celebrate this wonderful occasion we will have a number of exciting challenges and innovations ahead of us, including a round in Russia, the first-ever on the international motorsports calendar, plus a major championship identity rebranding scheme.

But for the moment it just remains for us to thank teams, riders, manufacturers, sponsors, partners, media and spectators for all their efforts and contributions this year and hope that you enjoy this comprehensive look back at the season in the official 2011 Superbike Yearbook.

See you again soon at the opening round in Australia!

Paolo and Maurizio Flammini

THAT'S SBK

One strong point of the Superbike World Championship has always been its rapport with the fans. Access to the paddock allows race-going spectators to enter in direct contact with the riders who always willingly lend themselves to this type of activity.

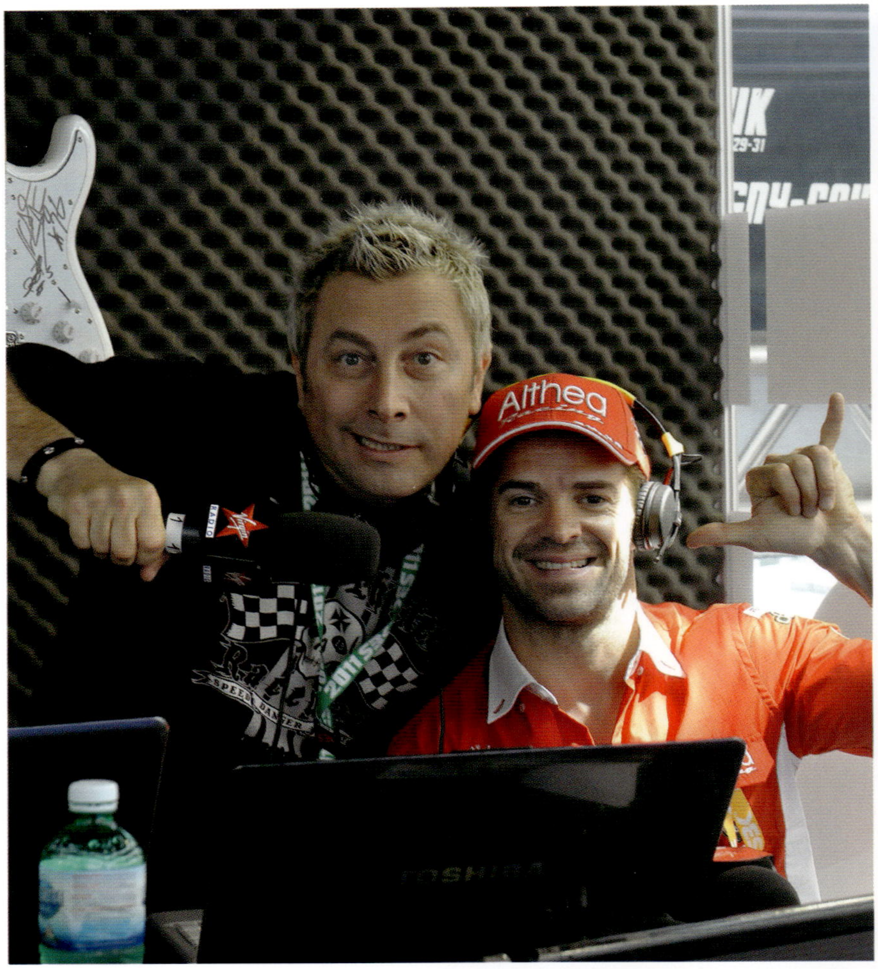
Althea

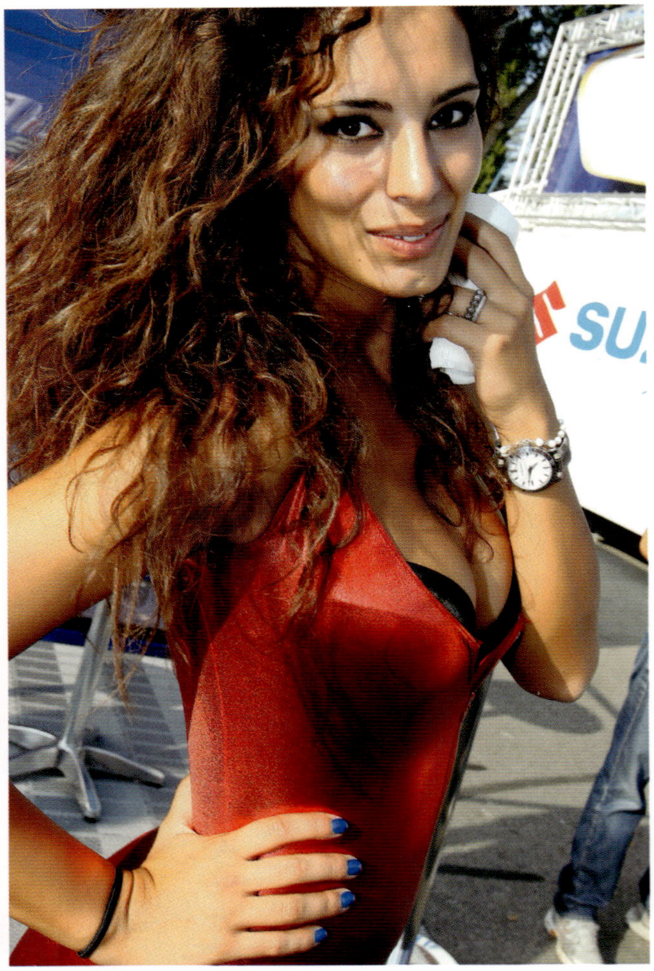

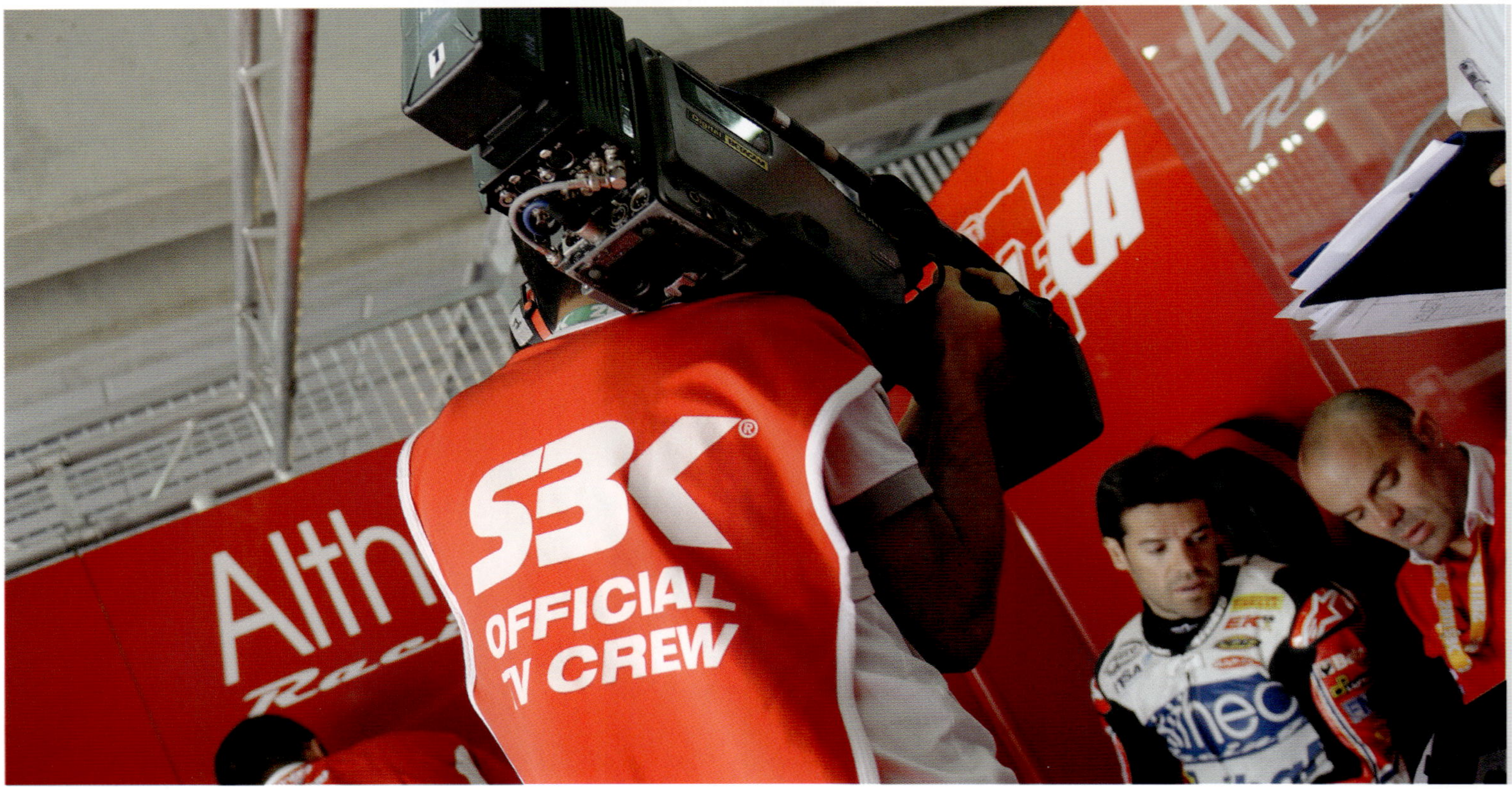
SBK
OFFICIAL

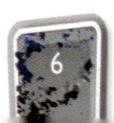

THAT'S SBK

After 24 years it's difficult to describe what Superbike is. Not because there are no or very few elements to go on but possibly for the entirely opposite reason.

Since the early days the Superbike World Championship has always revolved around contact between circuit-going fans and the riders on the track. In an increasingly inaccessible racing world, Superbike always remains accessible to everyone and even riders who in other championships may have been holed up in their pit garages or motorhomes, have easily made the transition to meet up with fans and the general public.

But the main characteristic of Superbike is the rapport between riders and teams, a rapport that is based on a certain type of social networking that results in convivial evenings in front of a plate of pasta in the paddock hospitality units or a chat with a beer or a glass of wine. Something that is very rare to find in other sporting disciplines.

All this can be found within the framework of a championship that sees the presence of seven different manufacturers on the starting-grid, a true demonstration of the importance of a category that unites technical road-bike advancements with an original format based on Superpole and two races in each round.

And while riders and bikes do their best to render incandescent the atmosphere at every round, the championship promoters always have one eye on the race-going public by organizing moments of entertainment such as the traditional press conferences held after Superpole and every race on the Paddock Show stage, another of World Superbike's assets.

It's all embellished by splendid grid-girls, ultra high-tech bikes and some of the fastest riders on the planet who continue to make every edition of the Superbike World Championship as fascinating as ever. But what counts more than words or pictures, is being there at least once a year...

Once they step off their bikes and take off their helmets the protagonists of Superbike, riders born exclusively to go at 300 km/h, mingle with the crowds in the paddock who themselves are often worth meeting…

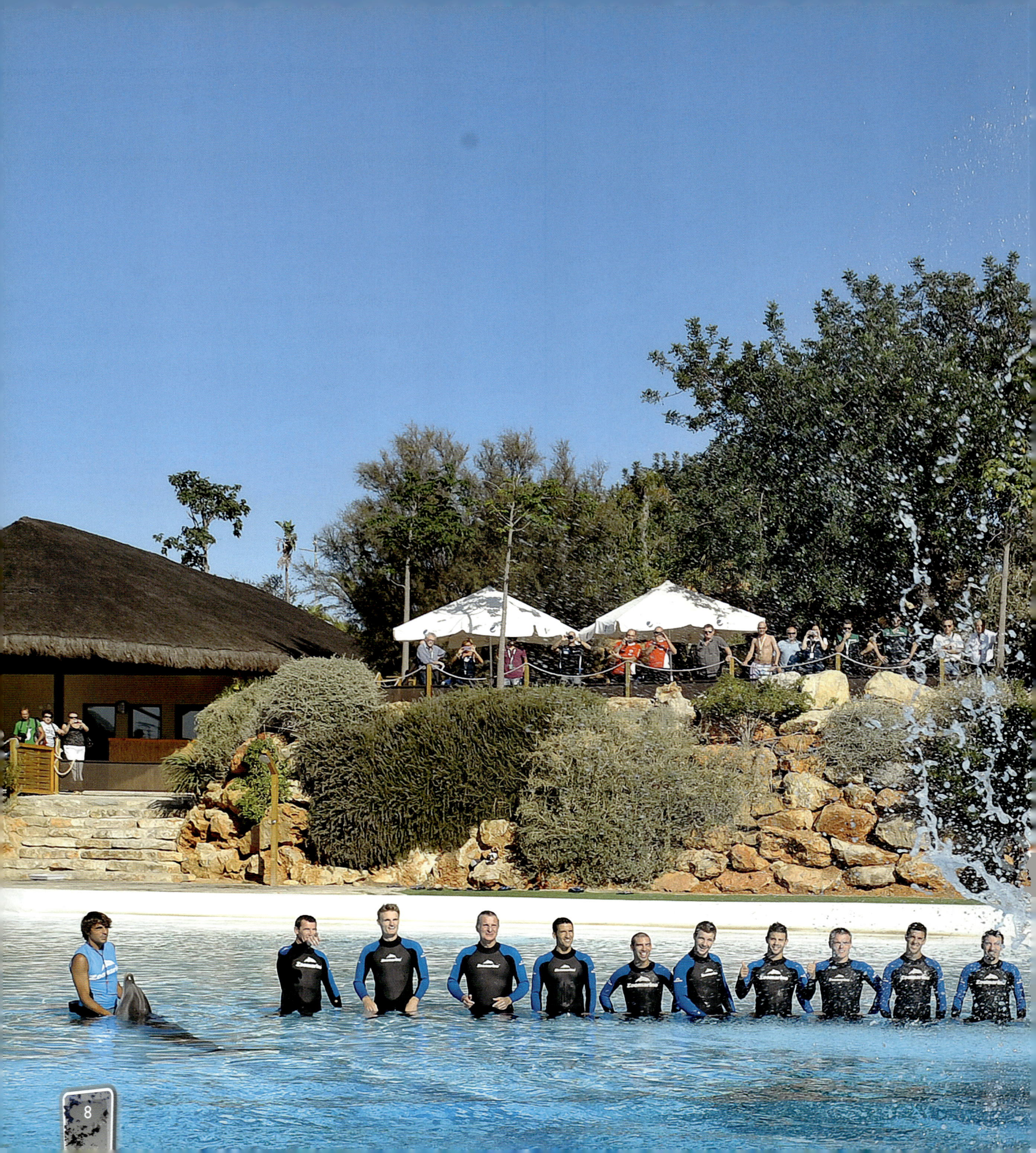

Men, machines, technology, excitement: an explosive mix that lies at the basis of the success of World Superbike. It's not only about the men and the machines but also about putting on a show to conquer new spectators both in circuits and in front of the TV screens.

But Superbike is also about thrills and above all surprises. Sometimes pleasant surprises such as the Misano round where the pit straight of the circuit was the scene for a memorable gala evening in which riders, team members, sponsors, partners and media were wined, dined and entertained in an unusual but fascinating setting, as can be seen in this night-time view of the event.

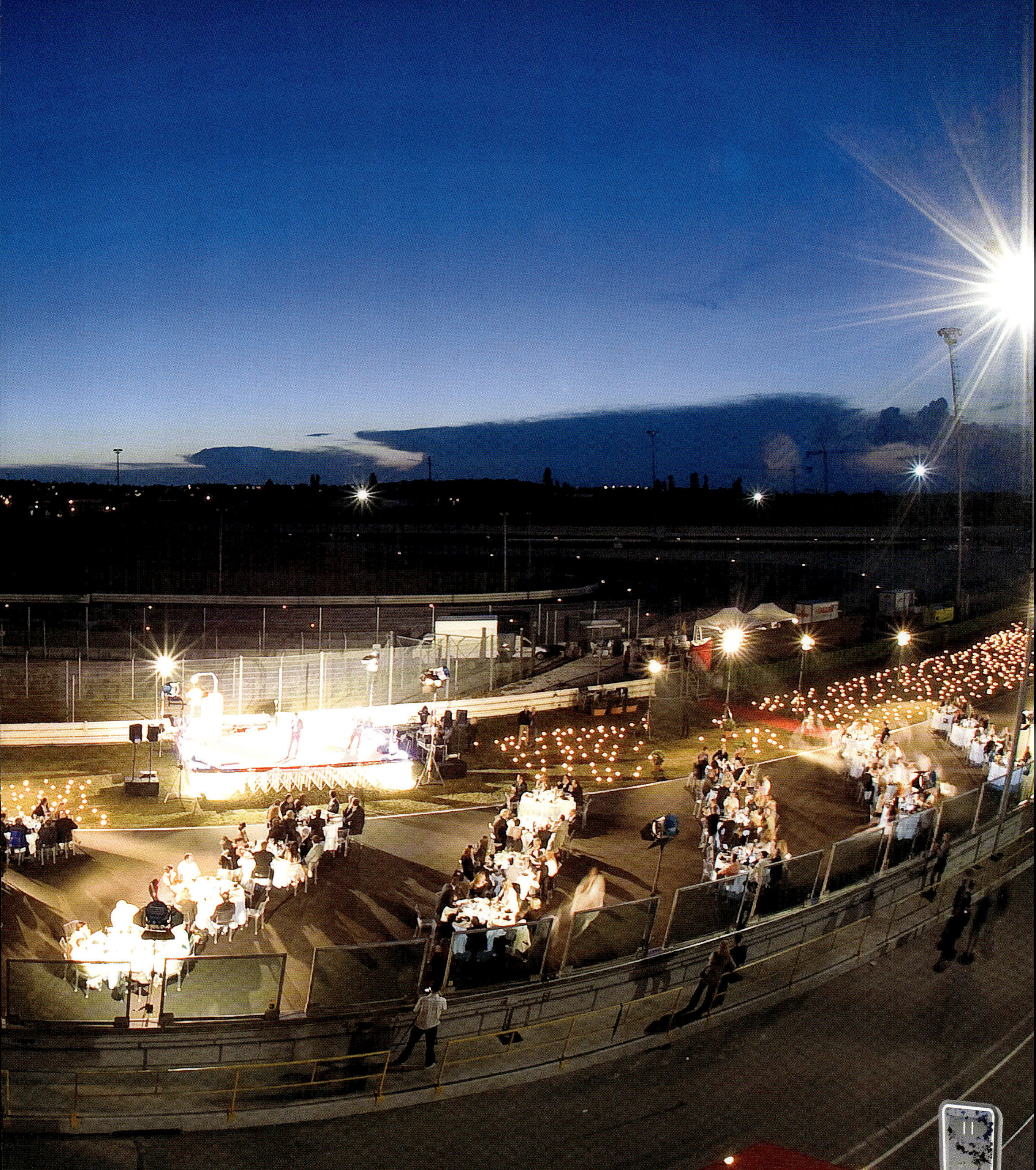

infront

1
APRILIA ALITALIA RACING TEAM
2010
SUPERBIKE WORLD CHAMPION
aprilia

YAMAHA
AW-750-RE

SUPERBIKE
FIM WORLD CHAMPIONSHIP
FIM
TISSOT

ALFA ROMEO

SBK SUPERBIKE
FIM WORLD CHAMPIONSHIP

THAT'S SBK

The world of Superbike is also a place where the protagonists can get together, not only during event presentations and press conferences but also in the evening with a beer or a glass of wine in hand.

SBK‹‹
SUPERBIKE
FIM WORLD CHAMPIONSHIP

AN EXCITING NEW IDENTITY
COMING IN 2012

WORLDSBK‹.COM

PURE MOTORSPORT

WSBK CHAMPION

CARLOS CHECA

18

WSBK CHAMPION

Carlos Checa's title win in this year's Superbike World Championship was greeted positively by almost everyone; a unanimous consensus that is not always present in racing, even in the production-based Superbike series, which is generally known for having good rider relations.

The overriding conclusion seemed to be that "If I can't win the title, then I don't mind if Carlos wins it". In fact the man from Sant Fruitos de Bages near Barcelona is undoubtedly one of the nicest and most easy-going guys in the Superbike paddock and this enables him to get on well with all the other riders, albeit with the regulation dose of healthy rivalry.

The title won in his fourth season in World Superbike was the crowning glory in the long career of Carlos, who for many years was one of the leading riders in 500 and in MotoGP, and then continued to be so in the production-based series.

Before 2011 many of his detractors said that Carlos would never win a title but they failed to appreciate what Checa had become in 2010, when he worked a lot on his mental training. This not only allowed him to deal with stiff opposition from riders of the calibre of Max Biaggi and Marco Melandri but also to overcome difficult moments such as the crash at Motorland Aragon which hampered his path towards the world title.

It proved that victory in the World Championship did not come about through a series of lucky circumstances but because of Carlos' terrific form. As well as having an excellent ability to manage qualifying and race strategy, it should also be pointed out that the

Carlos Checa's riding style this year was almost impeccable, with just one error at Motorland Aragon that jeopardized his march towards the crown. After the Spanish Round the Althea man kept his cool and put his title challenge back on the rails again.

ITSA
Althea
Unibat
DUCATI

Unibat
CHECA

Althea
Unibat
CHECA

SUPERBIKE
WORLD CHAMPIONSHIP

WSBK CHAMPION

Spaniard had a perfect feeling with his Ducati 1098R machine. And the difference could be seen in the performance of the other Ducati riders, who were never able to obtain the same results as Carlos.

Checa's title was not 'gifted' to him, because the thorns in his side came from four other winners, Marco Melandri, Max Biaggi, Eugene Laverty and Jonathan Rea, who however were unable to prevent him from notching up a total of 15 race wins. Those wins came from just six pole positions, demonstrating that the Spaniard always concentrated on scoring the best result in the race rather than in qualifying.

Last, but not least, was the perfect feeling reached with the team that gave him vital support and back-up throughout the year, a feeling that was rewarded with gratitude and a strong team spirit and confirmed during the end-of-season contract stand-off. In his second year with the Althea Racing team, Carlos could count on an expert and perfectly amalgamated group of team members, despite them hailing from different backgrounds of experience. The key elements of the team that had worked together for years were flanked by the Ducati engineers who had followed the latest evolution version of the 1198. And this harmony undoubtedly helped to tranquillize Checa, who was able to fully focus on winning the world title.

But the benefits were not simply one-way: in fact Checa's character was also fully in line with the members of the team once he was off the bike. This is another aspect of Carlos Checa's success, something that goes far beyond the mere sporting achievement of winning 15 races throughout the year and putting a gap of more than 100 points between himself and his closest rivals.

At 39 years of age Carlos Checa has proved to be a very strong rider, one who is capable of managing difficult situations and the high tension of the races thanks to a perfect knowledge of the bike and the tyres that allow him to make the most of the material available in the best possible way and time.

One of the strong features of Carlos Checa's 2011 season was undoubtedly the Spanish rider's rapport with his team. Althea Racing was made up of some of the squad's long-term members flanked by Ducati engineers working with the Civita Castellana-based team.

X-lite
X-802
ITSA
FMA
LighTech
Unibat
Althea
Althea Racing
DUCATI
1198
Unibat Batterie
FMA
PIRELLI

WSBK RIDERS

AKRAPOVIĆ
F.FABBRI
ACCESSORI
rizoma
AKRAPOVIC
domino
YAMAHA
X-802
FERODO
がんばろう日

MONSTER ENERGY
PIRELLI
YAMAHA
SPIDI
NOLAN
PIRELLI
YAMAHA
SUPERBIKE

WSBK RIDERS

Even in a season which saw Carlos Checa (Ducati) win the title in dominant fashion, there was no lack of talented competition to further raise the profile and quality of the 2011 World Superbike Championship.

The Spaniard's biggest adversaries were, without doubt, Marco Melandri and Max Biaggi. The former was making his Superbike debut this year, after having won a 250cc GP title and several MotoGP races earlier in his career. He was immediately up to speed on his Yamaha, and thanks to his considerable experience, he quickly learned to use the new tires and make the most of the Superbike formula. And he managed to catch on so fast that he scored a win in only the second round, and third race, that he was competing in. Donington Park was the scene of his first victory, which would later be joined by another three, at Aragon, Brno and Portimao. "Macho" – a nickname given to him by fans – exchanged second place in points with Max Biaggi for most of the season, and in the end, thanks also to the Aprilia rider's injury, Melandri eventually finished as the runner-up to Checa. The defending World Champion, coming off an excellent 2010 season, had to wait until Motorland Aragon race 2 before he could stand on the top step of the podium, showing just how quickly things can change in Superbike. Biaggi scored eight second place finishes, and he was a title threat to Checa all the way through the Brno round, up until his incredibly injury at the Nurburgring. As is well known, Max fractured his left foot when it was randomly struck by a sewer grate, sidelining him for three rounds of the championship, and ending not only any chance of defending his title, but also any possibility of fighting for second place in points.

Making his World Superbike debut, Marco Melandri (33) finished an impressive second in championship points, beating out Max Biaggi (1), with whom he had several exciting battles. The Yamaha rider reacted professionally to the news that the official team would be pulling out of the series. He will race a factory BMW for 2012.

27

Trying to win a second consecutive title was Apriliar rider Max Biaggi. The reigning World Champion had to deal with some very agreesive copetition, and his incredible injury at the Nurburgring ended any hopes he had of a late charge.

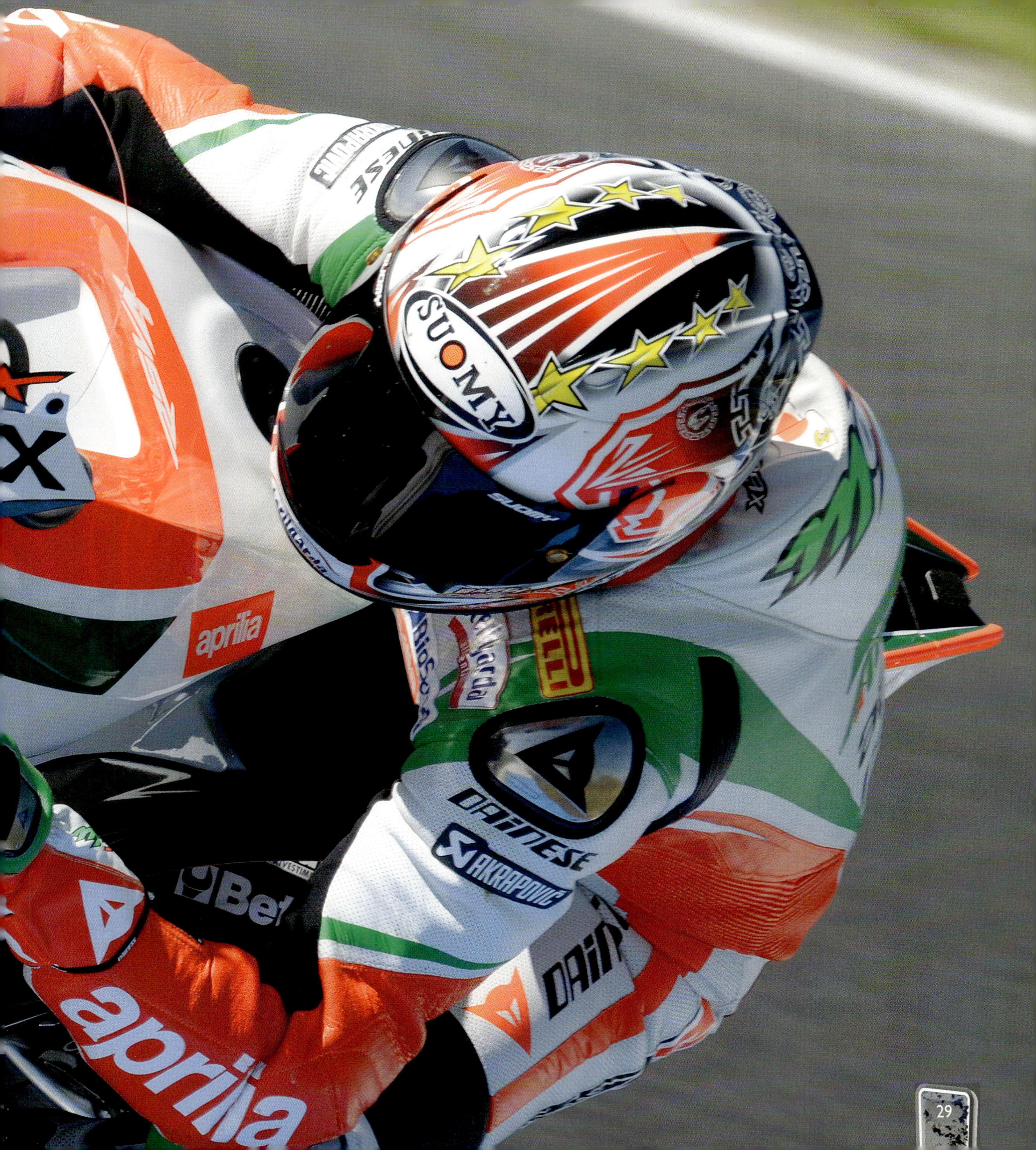
SUOMY
aprilia
DAINESE
AKRAPOVIC
aprilia

WSBK RIDERS

It was a positive season overall for Leon Haslam (91) in his first year at BMW. The British rider finished fifth in championship points. Another World Superbike rookie, Eugene Laverty (58), scored a double win at Monza.

Episodes like those from Donington Park and Monza (where he received penalties form Race Direction) also played their part in "disturbing" his championship rhythm, despite the competitiveness of his Aprilia.

Another bike capable of fighting with the Ducati for wins was the Yamaha, which added another two wins to Melandri's total of four, thanks to the superb riding of Eugene Laverty. The Irishman, also contesting his rookie World Superbike season, showed no fear in the face of more experienced and celebrated competition. As a matter of fact, Laverty often fought on equal terms with Checa, Biaggi and Melandri, with a fourth place championship finish to show for his efforts.

Speaking of putting in an effort, the considerable commitment shown all season by Leon Haslam is certainly worth highlighting. The British rider, who was the runner-up in the 2010 championship, was spending his first season aboard a BMW, a motorcycle with considerable potential, but not quite fully refined yet. Leon managed to get on the podium three times with the German four-cylinder machine, a very consistent championship that saw him scoring points in almost every round. This sustained speed was enough to earn Haslam fifth in the overall championship standings.

It was a season of constant growth for Sylvain Guintoli, who joined World Superbike in 2010 (finishing seventh). After a move from Suzuki to Ducati, the Frenchman – aside from a third place finish in Salt Lake City – didn't particularly impress early in the year. From Silverstone onward, however, he began to record a string of better results (like his second place finishes at the Nurburgring and Portimao), which eventually added up to sixth place in the final points tally.

Despite having two very capable Aprilias at

SHOEI
58
domino
YAMAHA
WITH YOU JAPAN
がんばろう日本
R1
PIRELLI
YAMAHA
YAMALUBE
PIRELLI

32

Two race wins was the final tally for Jonathan Rea (4), hampered by an injury suffered during the Misano morning warm up session. The eventual use of a ride by wire throttle on his Honda allowed him to compete on equal terms with his competition later in the season.

WSBK RIDERS

their disposal, both Leon Camier and Noriyuki Haga failed to demonstrate their true potential. The former, riding a full factory bike, scored one second and three third place results, certainly below expectations for his second season on the Italian machine. The Japanese rider was staggeringly inconsistent, alternating good results with races where he was totally invisible. His best round of the year came at Imola, where he twice finished second on the team PATA Racing Aprilia.

There were certainly high expectations for Jonathan Rea before the season started, but despite his two wins at Assen and Imola, the British rider could manage no better than ninth in points. The Castrol Honda rider's season was marked by two key events: his crash and injury in the morning warm up at Misano, which caused him to miss four rounds of the championship; and the adoption of a ride by wire system for the final races of the season, which drastically increased the performance of his CBR 1000 RR.

Making a return to World Superbike – and riding a competitive bike for the first time - Ayrton Badovini managed to crack the top ten in overall points, thanks to a middle part of his season where he recorded a series of solid finishes.

Also having an overall positive Superbike debut was Spanish rider Joan Lascorz, who ended up as the best of the Kawasaki riders. Although his teammate Tom Sykes managed to win a wild race at the Nurburgring (run under incredibly heavy rain), the superior consistency of Lascorz allowed him to come out on top (in eleventh place). Nevertheless, Sykes once again demonstrated his considerable potential.

Up through the round at Brno, Michel Fabrizio managed to score some satisfying results on his Suzuki – landing on the podium at Monza – but from Silverstone onward he really began to struggle. His downward slide was so drastic that he eventually fell to twelfth in championship points. Lastly, a note on the final season of World Superbike competition for Troy Corser, as the 40 year old decided to retire from racing and take on a test rider role for BMW.

Sylvain Guintoli (50) developed a good feeling with his Ducati in the second half of the year. Leon Camier (above left) finsihed seventh in championship points, just ahead of Noriyuki Haga (41). Tom Sykes (66) won a single race on his Kawasaki, at the Nurburgring under heavy rainfall.

35

WSBK RACES

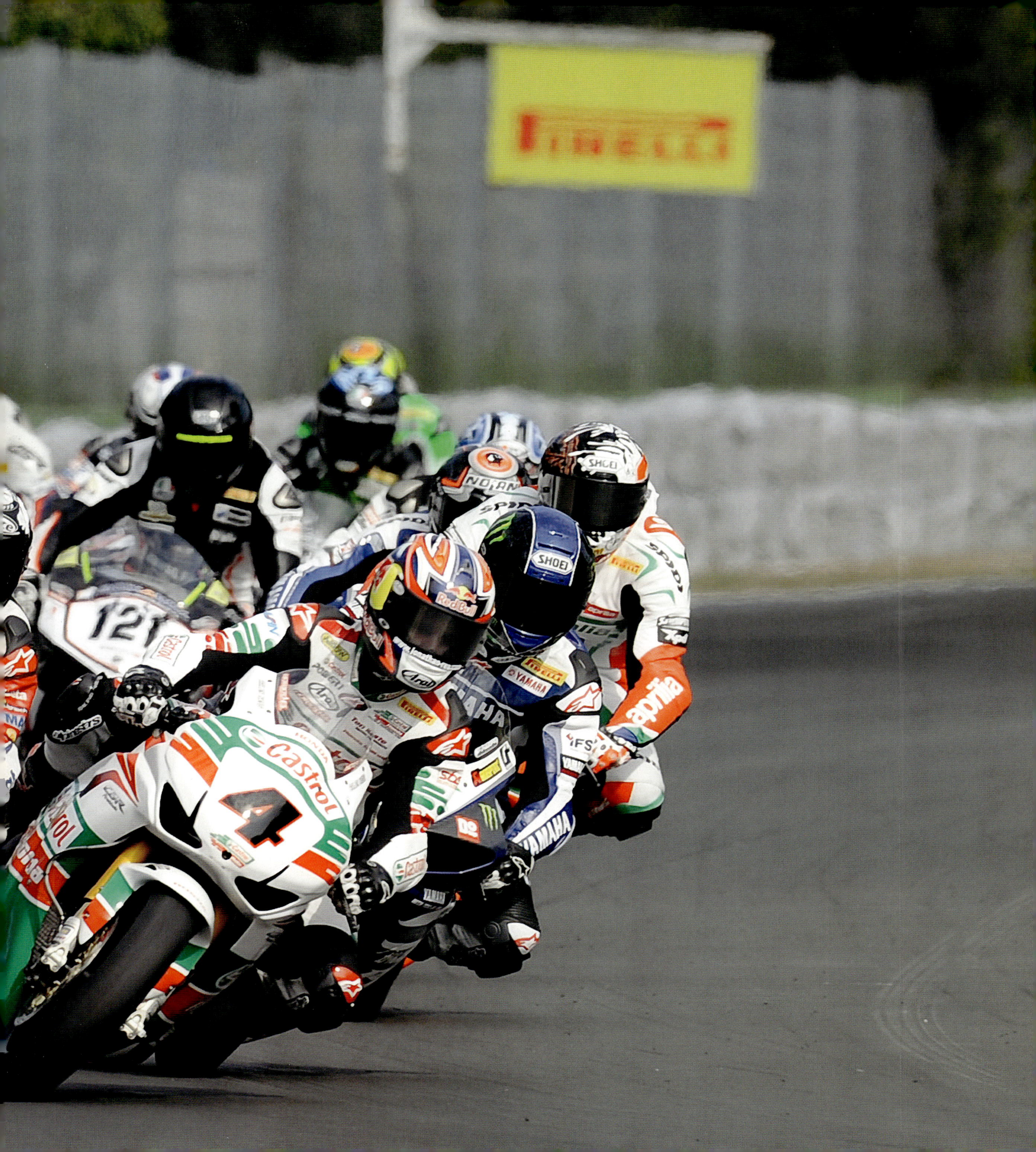
PIRELLI
121
SHOEI
Red Bull
Castrol
4
YAMAHA
aprilia

AUSTRALIA

PHILLIP ISLAND | 27•02

It was expected to be a duel between Max Biaggi, the reigning world champion, and Carlos Checa, the protagonist of the winter test sessions. And this was the case at least in Superpole, where the two were separated by only 13/1000 in favor of Spaniard, while the rest of the field seemed unable to challenge them. In the race the situation took a different turn, as Checa did not leave much room for his opponents, inflicting a heavy blow in the first race of the season. Old controversy came to light regarding the relative engine sizes and weights of the twins and four-cylinders, but it was the rider, bike and team combination that really made the difference. Further proof came from the fact that the top five in both races saw - apart from Checa's Ducati - only four-cylinder machines.

The final result in Australia was therefore a double win for Carlos Checa, placing him in the championship lead with maximum points, followed by Max Biaggi – running the number 1 on the fairing of his Aprilia for the first time in WSBK – who realized that two second place finishes were the best possible results. In race 1 Max was uncontested in second, while in race 2 he had to fight off Marco Melandri, making his debut in Superbike. Melandri already looked comfortable with his new bike, but he must also get to grips with new tires and especially with the formula, both in the form of Superpole (in which he was just twelfth) and the double race format.

Also showing well was Leon Haslam, the previous year's runner up, who debuted with BMW by scoring a podium in race 1 and in fifth place in race 2. Likewise, it was a strong Superbike debut for Eugene Laverty, who was fourth in race 1, but unfortunately ran long in race 2, compromising his finishing position.

Fighting hard for the podium in race 1 was Michel Fabrizio, in his first contest aboard the Alstare Suzuki, where the Roman started from the third row and eventually lost out in a tough scrap with Melandri and Laverty. In the second race he lost contact with the lead group early on, but was nevertheless happy with eighth place.

Kawasaki came into the season opening round with high expectations, after debuting a brand new bike and performing well in winter testing, but Tom

Superpole

	C. Checa	(ESP - Ducati)	1'30.882
			176,074 km/h

Race 1

1°	C. Checa	(ESP - Ducati)	34'16.503
			171,186 km/h
2°	M. Biaggi	(ITA - Aprilia)	+ 4.365
3°	L. Haslam	(GBR - BMW)	+ 10.719
4°	E. Laverty	(IRL - Yamaha)	+ 11.266
5°	M. Melandri	(ITA - Yamaha)	+ 11"293

Fastest lap

2°	M. Biaggi	(ITA - Aprilia)	1'32.034
			173,871 km/h

Race 2

1°	C. Checa	(ESP - Ducati)	34'15.041
			171,308 km/h
2°	M. Biaggi	(ITA - Aprilia)	+ 1.188
3°	M. Melandri	(ITA - Yamaha)	+ 1.406
4°	J. Rea	(GBR - Honda)	+ 10.563
5°	L. Haslam	(GBR - BMW)	+ 10.885

Fastest lap

3°	M. Biaggi	(ITA - Aprilia)	1'32.012
			173,912 km/h

There isn't much to say about a double win - just look at the gaps to second place - as Carlos Checa openes the 2011 World Superbike season in style. The Spaniard reigned supreme on his team Althea Ducati.

SBK
PIRELLI
Althea Racing
Unibat
2011 SBK
Althea Racing
Unibat Batterie

40

Carlos Checa's triumphant weekend began with the Superpole, all under the watchful eyes of predecessor Troy Bayliss (above and center). There was little Marco Melandri and Max Biaggi could do to stop him (in the larger photo).

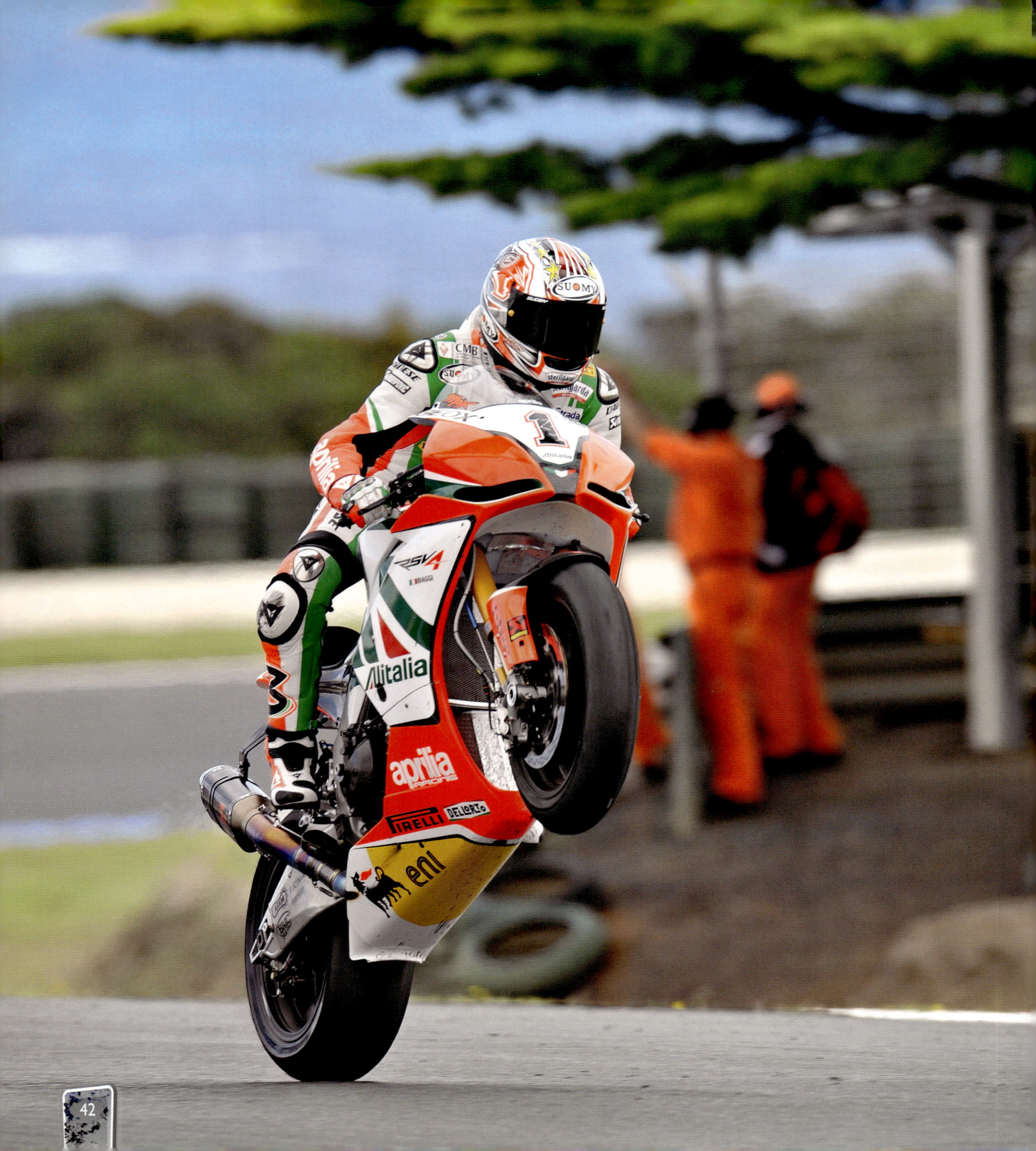
SUOMY
RSV4
Alitalia
aprilia
PIRELLI
DELLORTO
eni

WSBK RACES

Sykes could do no better than eighth and tenth place finishes.

Staying with the Japanese manufacturers, a fourth place in race 2, scored by Jonathan Rea, was the only bright spot of the weekend for Honda. The British rider displayed his usual determination throughout the event, but his teammate Ruben Xaus was well off the pace of the leaders. Ninth and seventh place finishes comprised the less than stellar debut for Noriyuki Haga on the team PATA Aprilia RSV4. The Japanese rider has past experience with four-cylinder machinery (Yamaha), but appeared out of sorts with the Italian bike.

And speaking of things Italian, also noteworthy was the debut of the BMW Motorrad Italia Team, who fielded James Toseland and Ayrton Badovini. The first was in search of redemption, while the second was simply looking to win a permanent place in Superbike.

Boosting the Australian contingent, both on track and off, was the presence of WSBK legend Troy Bayliss in the paddock, while Josh Waters, an Australian and Team Yoshimura Suzuki rider, managed to get into the points in race 2.

Max Biaggi began his title defense with a pair of second place finishes, racing for the first time with the number 1 plate. It was a positive BMW debut for Leon Haslam (91), whose race 1 podium leaves him optimistic about the season to come.

43

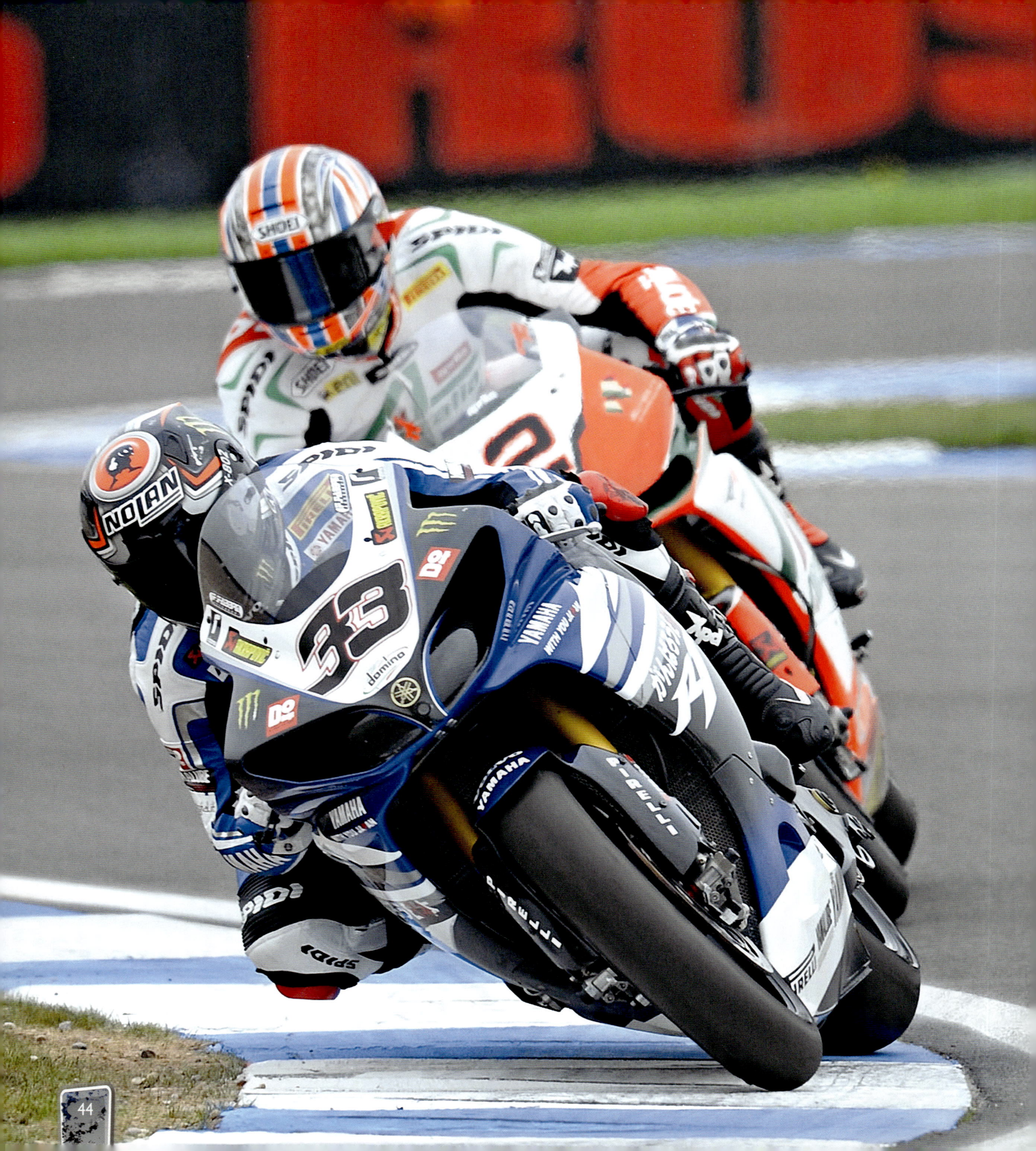
SHOEI
SPIDI
NOLAN
33
YAMAHA
PIRELLI
domino

EUROPE

DONINGTON PARK | 27•03

Superpole		
C. Checa	(ESP - Ducati)	1'28.099
		164,392 km/h

Race 1			
1°	M. Melandri	(ITA - Yamaha)	34'33.189
			160,672 km/h
2°	J. Smrz	(CZE - Ducati)	+ 2.455
3°	C. Checa	(ESP - Ducati)	+ 5.839
4°	L. Haslam	(GBR - BMW)	+ 6.176
5°	J. Rea	(GBR - Honda)	+ 9.039

Fastest lap			
3°	N. Haga	(JPN - Aprilia)	1'29.137
			162,478 km/h

Race 2			
1°	C. Checa	(ESP - Ducati)	34'21.537
			161,581 km/h
2°	M. Melandri	(ITA - Yamaha)	+ 3.397
3°	L. Camier	(GBR - Aprilia)	+ 5.902
4°	L. Haslam	(GBR - BMW)	+ 13.842
5°	J. Lascorz	(ESP - Kawasaki)	+ 14.253

Fastest lap			
8°	C. Checa	(ESP - Ducati)	1'28.988
			162,750 km/h

In only his second WSBK round, Marco Melandri (33, ahead of Leon Camier) shows how well he is adapting to the new series. The Italian scored his first win (and a second place finsih) at Donington Park, making himself a championship contender.

The World Superbike Championship returned to Europe at Donington Park, which had been left on the calendar the previous year, and without James Toseland, who crashed in testing at Motorland Aragon, suffering a broken wrist and right hand. Also highlighting the weekend were the numerous tributes to Japan, which was hit by a terrible earthquake and tsunami.

On a circuit that should have been unfavorable to the Ducati, Carlos Checa went against expectations and excelled in Superpole, ahead of Leon Haslam, Tom Sykes and the surprising Jakub Smrz. But the real protagonist (in the negative sense) of the day was Max Biaggi, who somehow managed to come into contact with Fabrizio, Haga and Melandri.

And it was the Yamaha rider who triumphed in race 1, in front of Czech rider Jakub Smrz, and Carlos Checa who, in turn, won race 2. The runner up in the second race was Melandri, who concluded an excellent British weekend considering it was only his second in the series. Among the most exciting moments from the round was the former 250cc champion's overtaking maneuver on Smrz - who had led the race for a long time – on the final lap.

Also standing out in race 1 was the comeback of Carlos Checa on Leon Haslam, who had actually led for some laps. The Englishman on the BMW can be quite happy, however, with a home race that saw him finish twice in fourth place, results that allowed him to stay third in the championship standings. On the other hand, it was another bad weekend at Donington for Max Biaggi. The Aprilia rider ran long and finished seventh in race 1, before receiving a black flag in race two. Max had failed to take his ride-through penalty for a jump start, resulting in his expulsion from the race.

"Macho" Melandri came home second in race two, following a good battle with Leon Camier, who was forced to settle for third.

Second place in race 1 went to Jakub Smrz, the first podium for team Effenbert - Liberty Racing, showing that the Czech rider isn't only fast in qualifying, but also over a race distance.

We finally saw a Kawasaki up amongst the leaders, and it was Spain's Joan Lascorz at the controls.

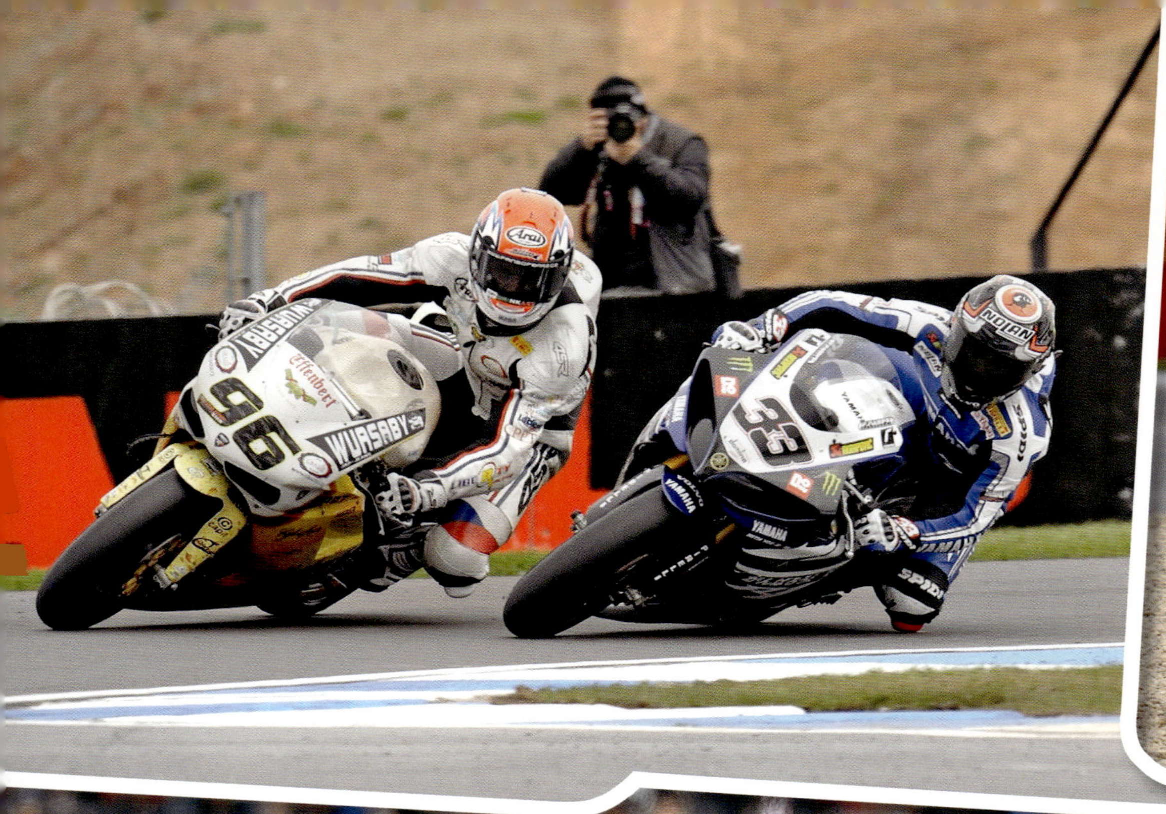
Arai
YAMAHA

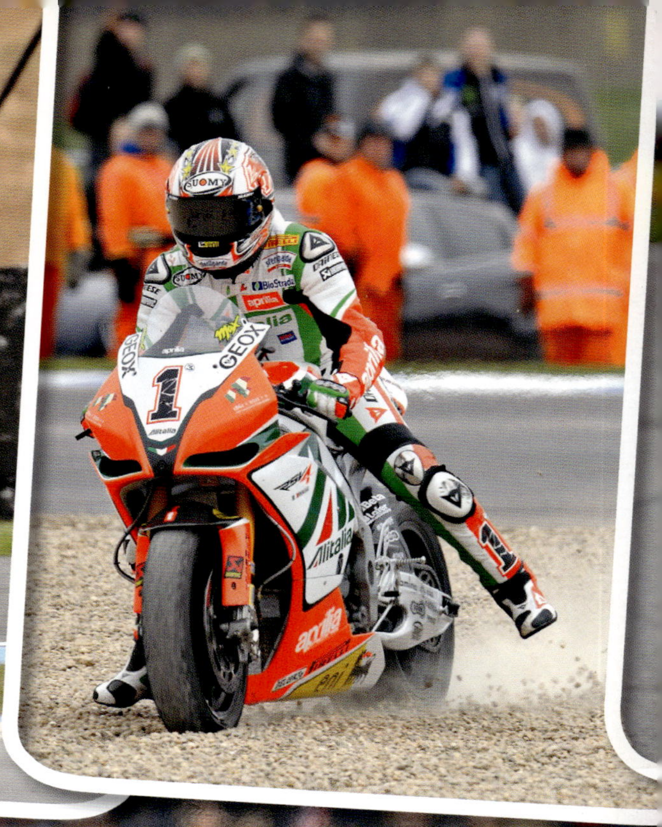
GEOX
Alitalia
aprilia

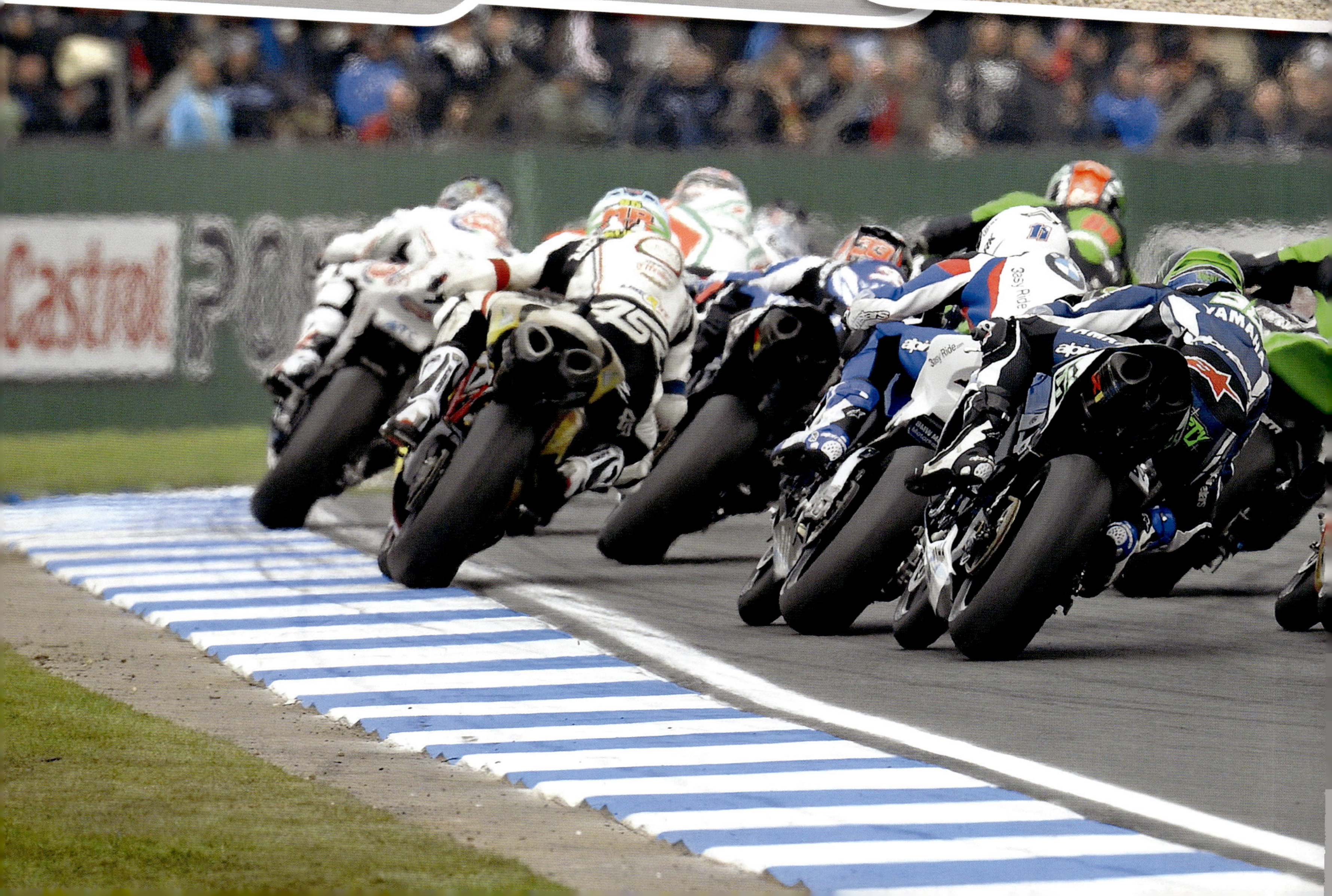
Castrol
YAMAHA

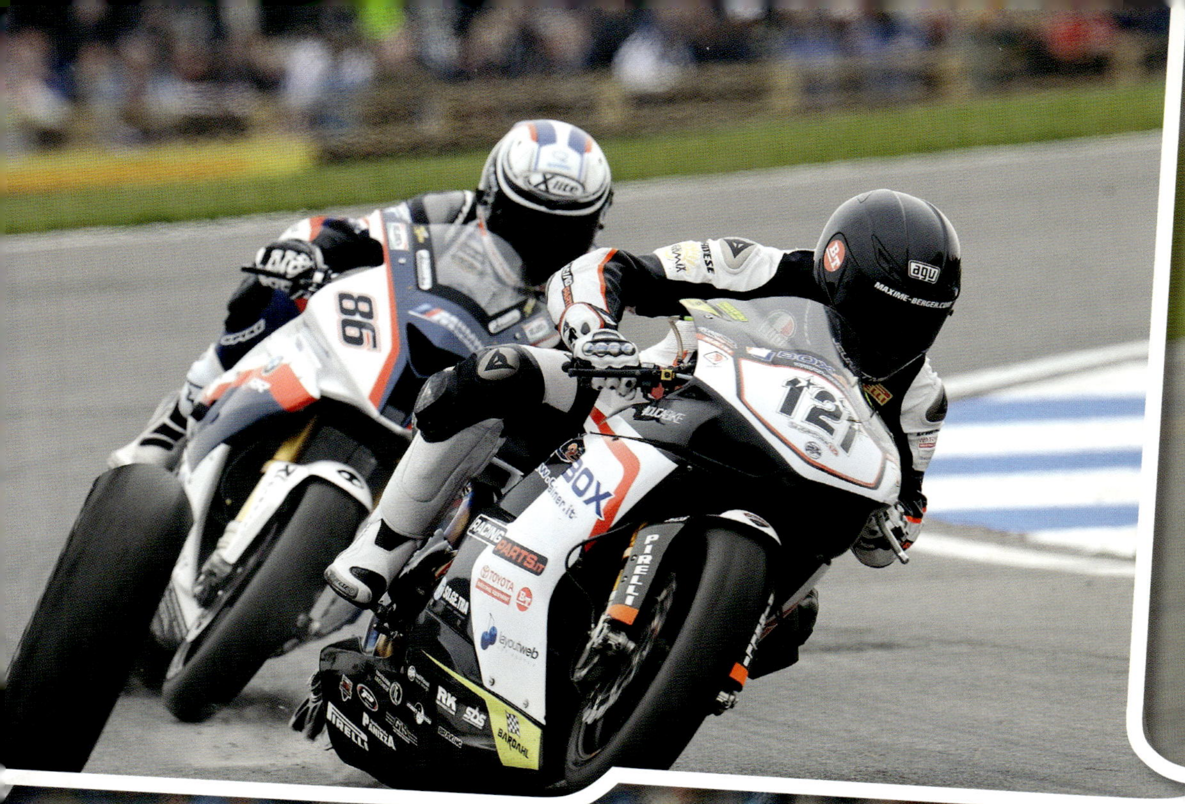
86
121
PIRELLI

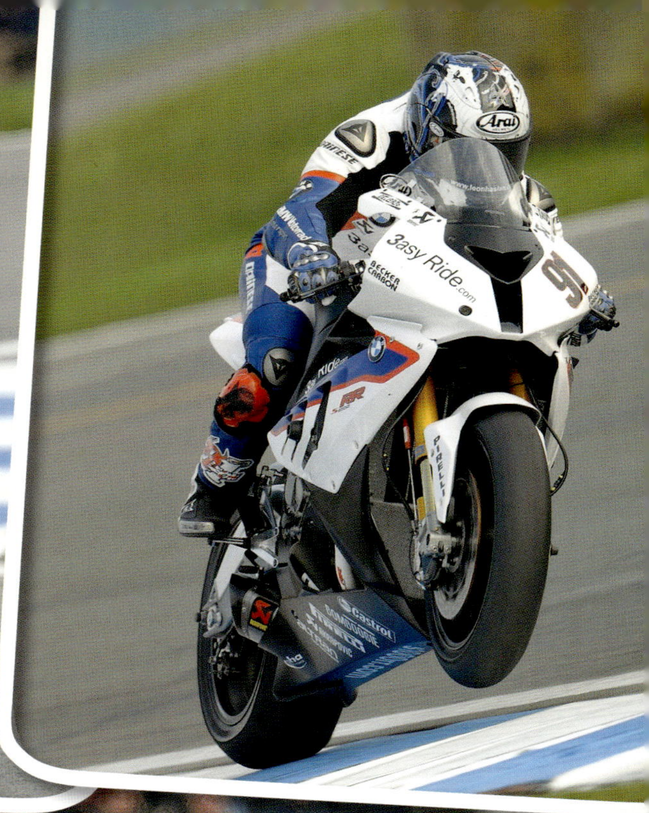
Arai

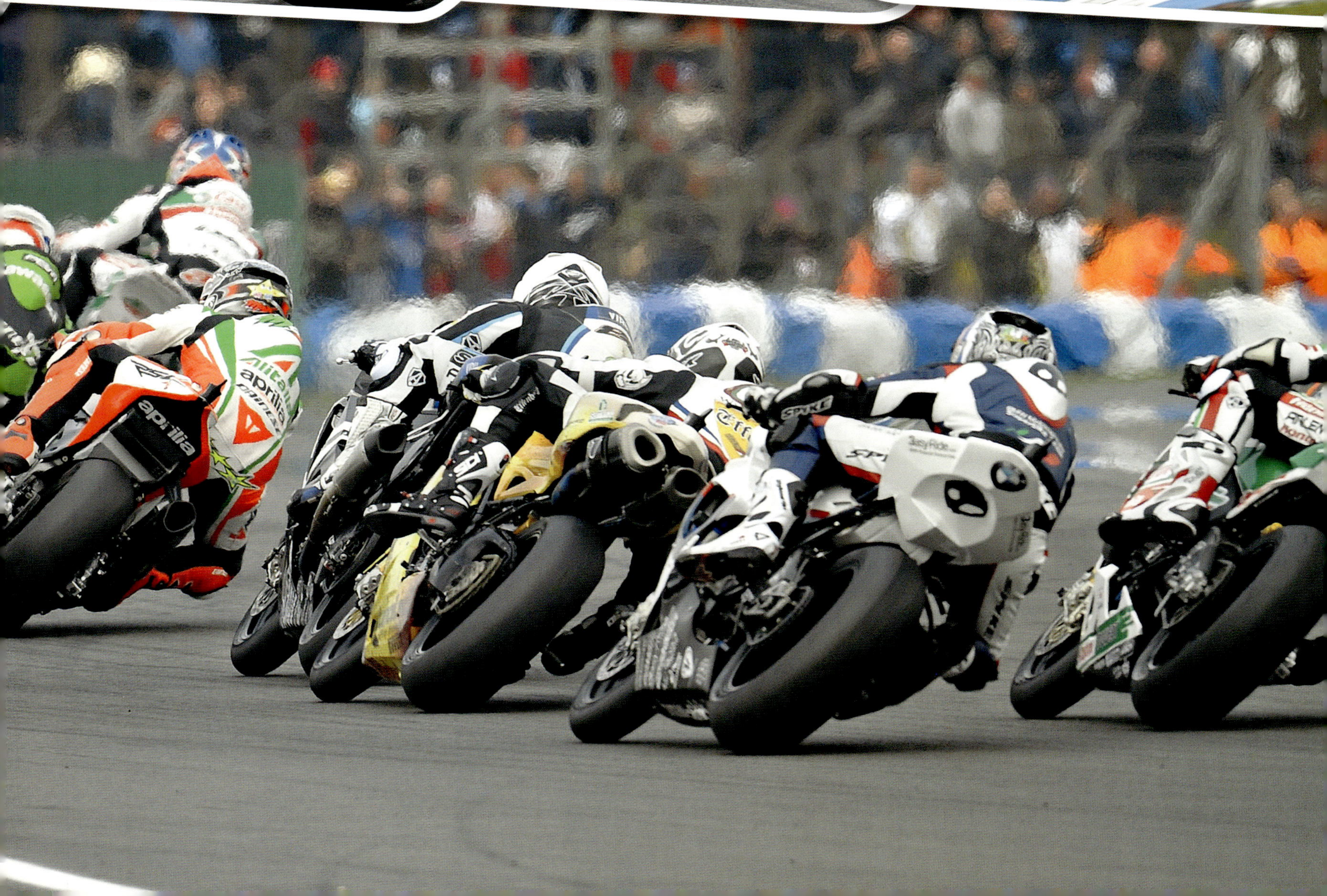
aprilia

WSBK RACES

Full of excitement, the Donington Park round saw Carlos Checa (7) triumph in race 2.
There were various tributes to Japan on display throughout the weekend, in honor the earthquake and tsunami victims.

The Spanish rookie finished race 2 in an encouraging fifth place.
Maxime Berger was the innocent victim of a spectacular, albeit harmless, incident in which the carbon fiber rear wheel of his Ducati failed, which provided another good scare for the fans and French rider alike.
Slightly overshadowed by the strong the strong home performances of Haslam and Camier was fellow British rider Jonathan Rea, who came away with fifth and sixth place finishes, a little below expectations for the Honda rider.
At this point in the championship, after two rounds and four races, Checa has a 21 point lead over Melandri and a 38 point gap over Haslam. Biaggi is 42 points behind, in fourth.

48

X-lite
SINCE 1972
DUCATI
Althea
Unibat
Batterie
FMA
1198
PIRELLI
DUCATI
maya design
BMP

NETHERLANDS

ASSEN | 17•04

That Carlos Checa managed to score his third Superpole in three races could have been a worrying sign for his competition, but they were probably still counting on the long duration of the championship to provide the necessary time to catch up to the rapid Spaniard.

At one of the most historic circuits on the World Superbike calendar (and for motorcycling in general), even with its recent modifications, we expected a strong reaction from Max Biaggi, as he looked to move past his forgettable Donnington weekend. The Roman was giving his best, but a crash in free practice caused some complications for his Superpole session, and he only qualified fifth fastest. Demonstrating good potential for the race were Jakub Smrz and Eugene Laverty, both looking to repeat their performances from the opening rounds, while Marco Melandri suffered a crash in Superpole.

Mixed among this group was Honda rider Jonathan Rea, who had recently carried out a series of tests at his team's home circuit, and whose pace race 1 proved untouchable for everyone.

Following the British rider across the line was Max Biaggi, who would repeat his second place performance in race 2, losing out to Carlos Checa by less than a second. The pair of strong results put Biaggi back into second place in the standings, an already significant 43 points behind the Ducati rider.

Checa was also the author of a heart-stopping pass on Biaggi in race 2, a move that would eventually prove decisive for his victory. Interestingly, the podiums for both races was made up of the same three names (Rea, Biaggi and Checa), even though their positions changed between the two events.

Leon Haslam gave fans a scare when he crashed amidst a group of riders in race 1, but the British rider rebounded with a strong fifth place finish in race 2, after battling with both Laverty and Fabrizio. The Suzuki rider was also a protagonist in race 1, having challenged Melandri for fourth place until the very last laps. And speaking of fourth place, in race 2 that position went to Leon Camier, the second of factory Aprilia riders, who struggled to match his teammates performances. Likewise, Noriyuki Haga struggled on his Aprilia, leaving the Dutch circuit with only an eighth place finish to his credit.

Race 2 didn't end in the best of ways for Melandri, as the Italian rider wound up in the gravel after battling with Jonathan Rea for third place.

Superpole

	C. Checa	(ESP - Ducati)	1'35.292
			171,590 km/h

Race 1

1°	J. Rea	(GBR - Honda)	35'46.486
			167,589 km/h
2°	M. Biaggi	(ITA - Aprilia)	+ 0.739
3°	C. Checa	(ESP - Ducati)	+ 3.572
4°	M. Melandri	(ITA - Yamaha)	+ 9.508
5°	M. Fabrizio	(ITA - Suzuki)	+ 9.892

Fastest lap

3°	T. Sykes	(GBR - Kawasaki)	1'36.660
			169,162 km/h

Race 2

1°	C. Checa	(ESP - Ducati)	35'38.693
			168,199 km/h
2°	M. Biaggi	(ITA - Aprilia)	+ 0.524
3°	J. Rea	(GBR - Honda)	+ 3.584
4°	L. Camier	(GBR - Aprilia)	+ 5.913
5°	L. Haslam	(GBR - BMW)	+ 16.916

Fastest lap

3°	L. Camier	(GBR - Aprilia)	1'36.476
			169,485 km/h

Taking his share of the World Superbike spotlight in the third round was Jonathan Rea, one of the most promising young riders in the series. The British rider managed to best Max Biaggi race one.

Red Bull
www.jonathan-rea.com
Arai
PIRELLI
Castrol
Honda
HONDA
Castrol
4

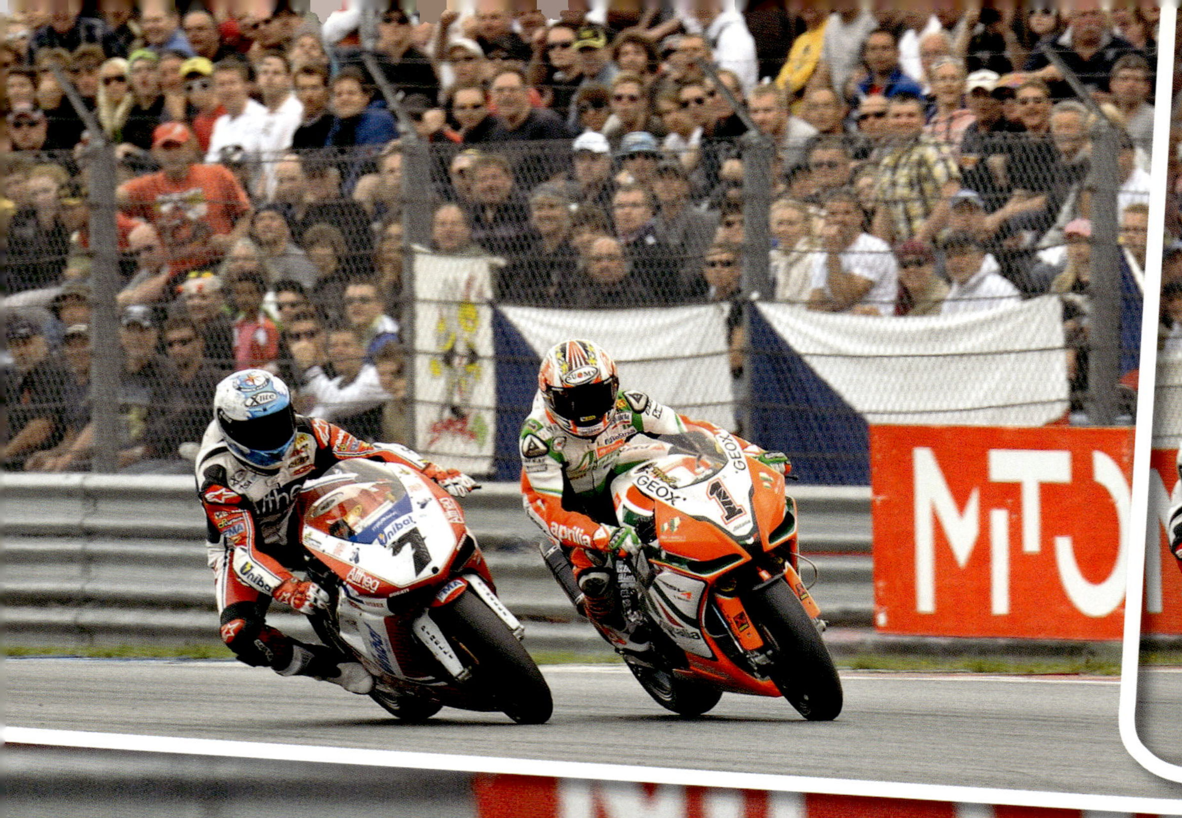

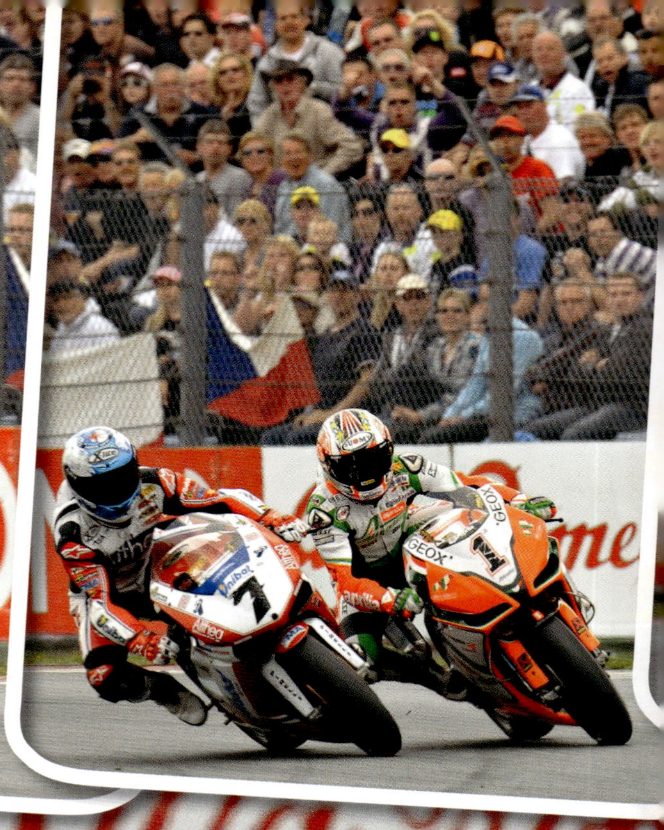

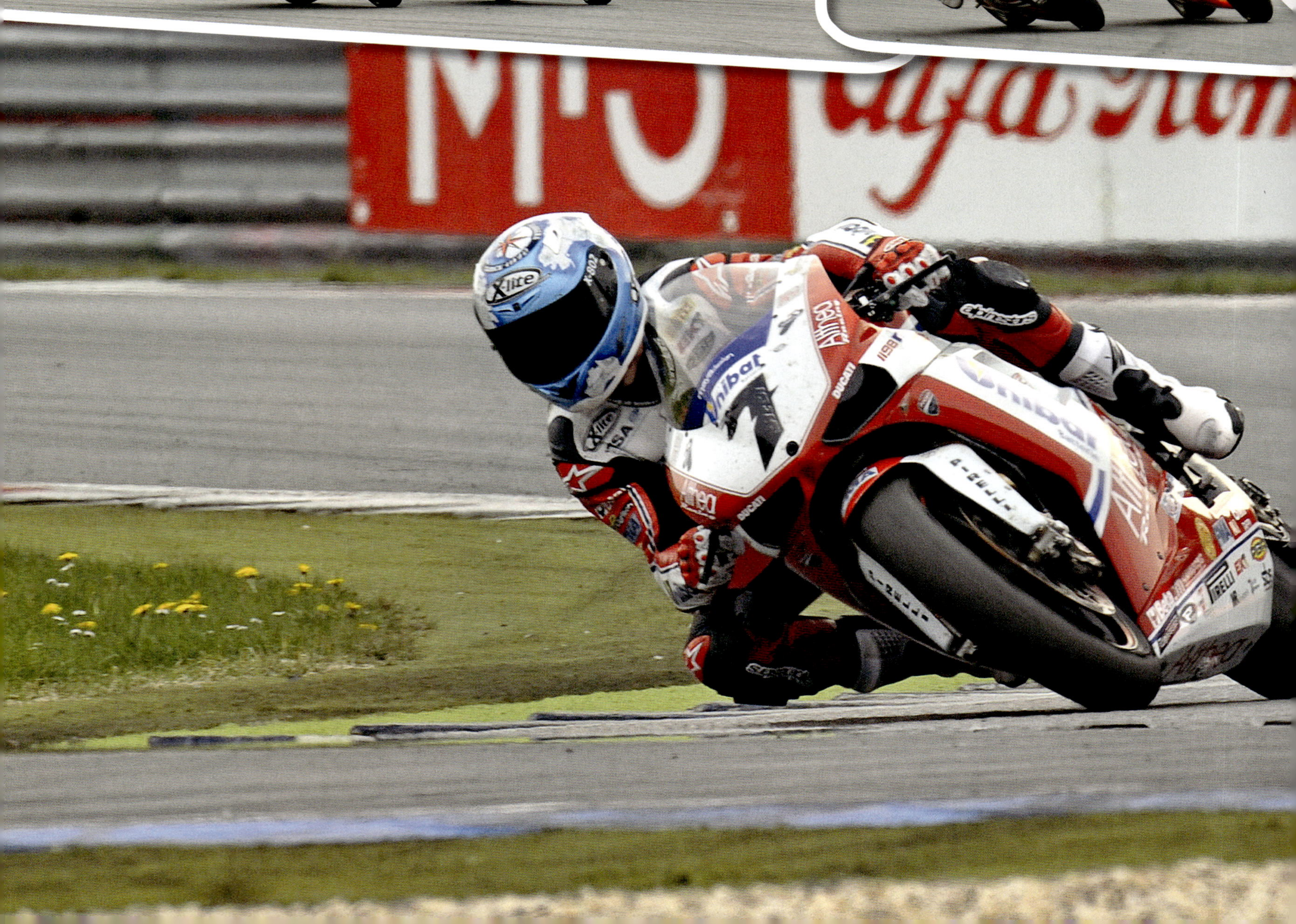

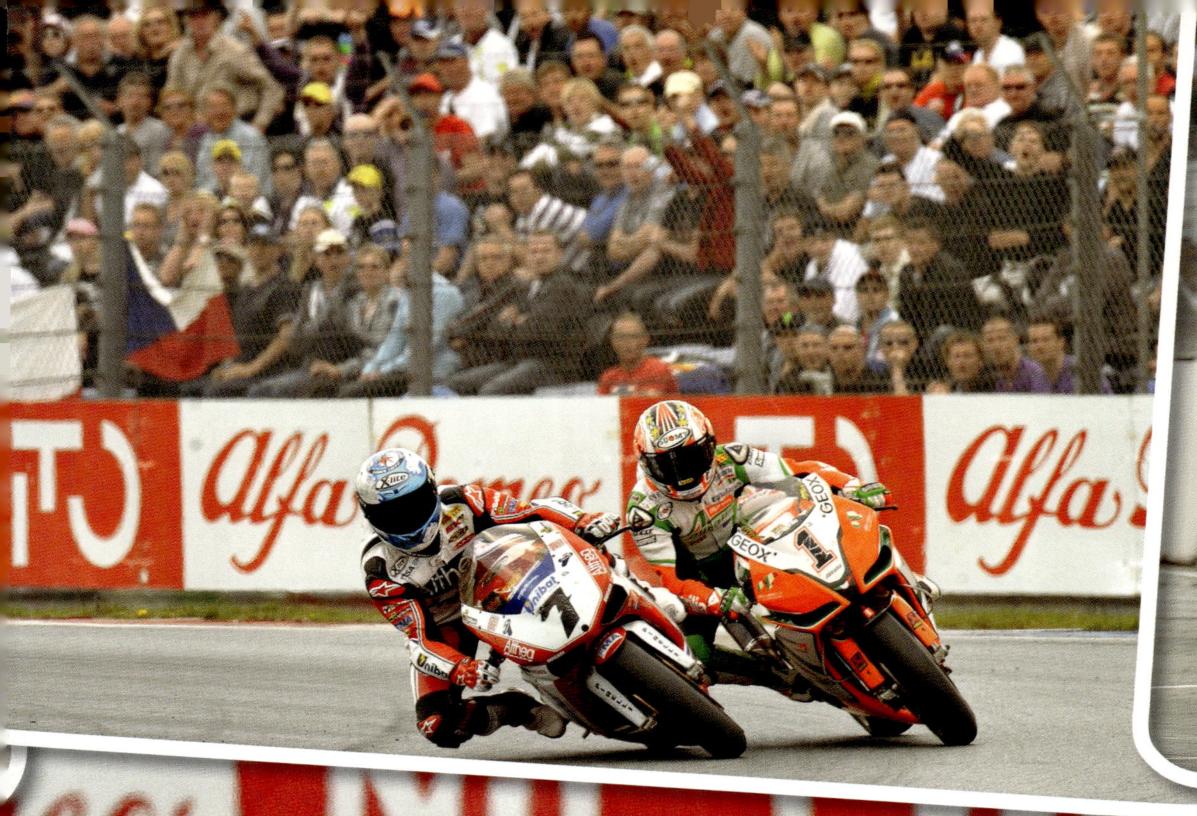

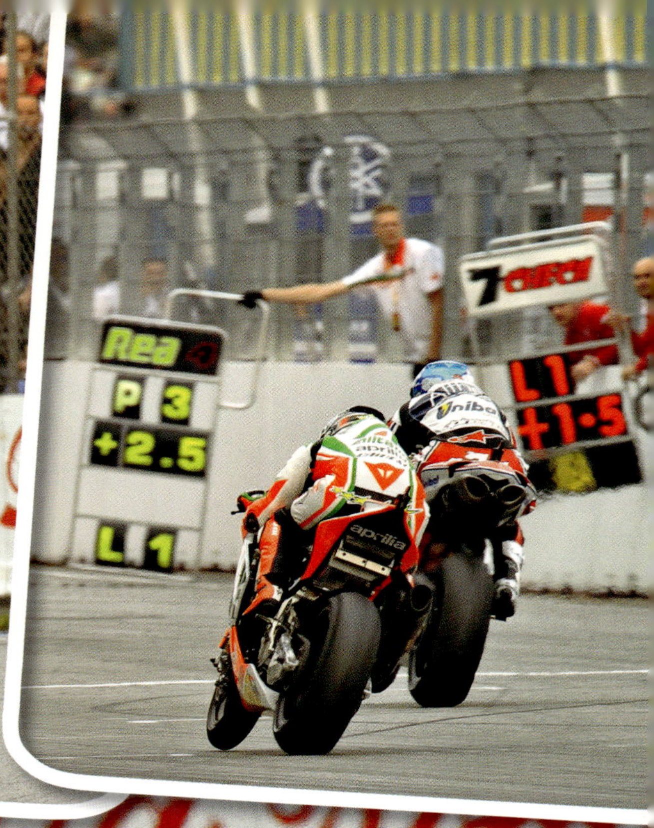
Rea
P 3
+2.5
L 1
L1
+1·5

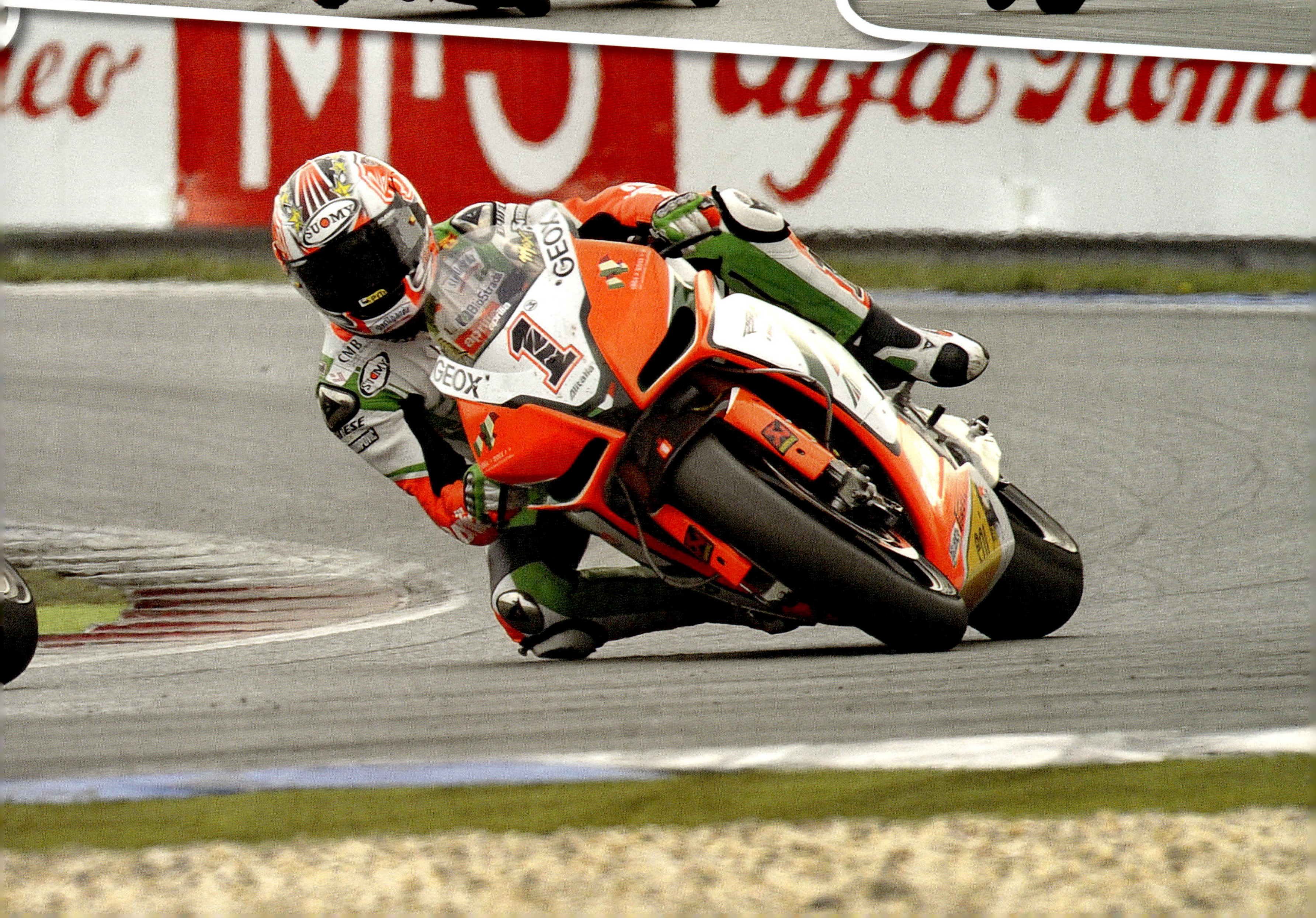

WSBK RACES

Marco Melandri (33) and Michel Fabrizio (84) found themselves fighting for position in race 1, while Carlos Checa stamped his authority on the day's second contest. Leon Camier (2) finished race 2 just off the podium.

Other highlights from the Assen races include a sixth place finish for Troy Corser, and a top ten result for Ayrton Badovini, who didn't seem overly affected by the pressure of leading the BMW Italia team, as a result of Toseland's absence. Taking the Briton's place for the round was home rider Barry Veneman, who put in an honest performance. Returning to action during the weekend was Chris Vermeulen, although the Australian rider could only manage to complete eight laps in race 1, before he called it a day.

Spicing up the show were crashes from both team Effenbert - Liberty Racing riders. Jakub Smrz "opened" the thottle a little too violently and wound up on the ground, while Sylvain Guintoli, who was following him, wound up crashing as he attempted to avoid his fallen teammate. Luckily neither rider was seriously injured, and both were able to start race 2 as planned.

Assen was a tough round for the Kawasaki riders, which actually saw Mark Aitchison use his team Pedercini bike to beat out factory mounted Joan Lascorz. The Australian is a rider of considerable potential, and although it isn't always realized, he never hesitates to fight for a good result whenever possible. Such was the case with his tenth place finish in Holland. In race 2, however, a technical issue forced him to make a pit stop, causing him to finish last. Tom Sykes could do no better, only managing an eleventh place finish in race 2.

The championship standings after Assen saw Carlos Checa leading with 132 points, versus Biaggi's 89, and Melandri's 85.

SBK
Althea
Racing
Unibat
Batterie
SBK
SBK

SPIDI
SHOEI
aprilia
Alitalia
eni
2

LAP

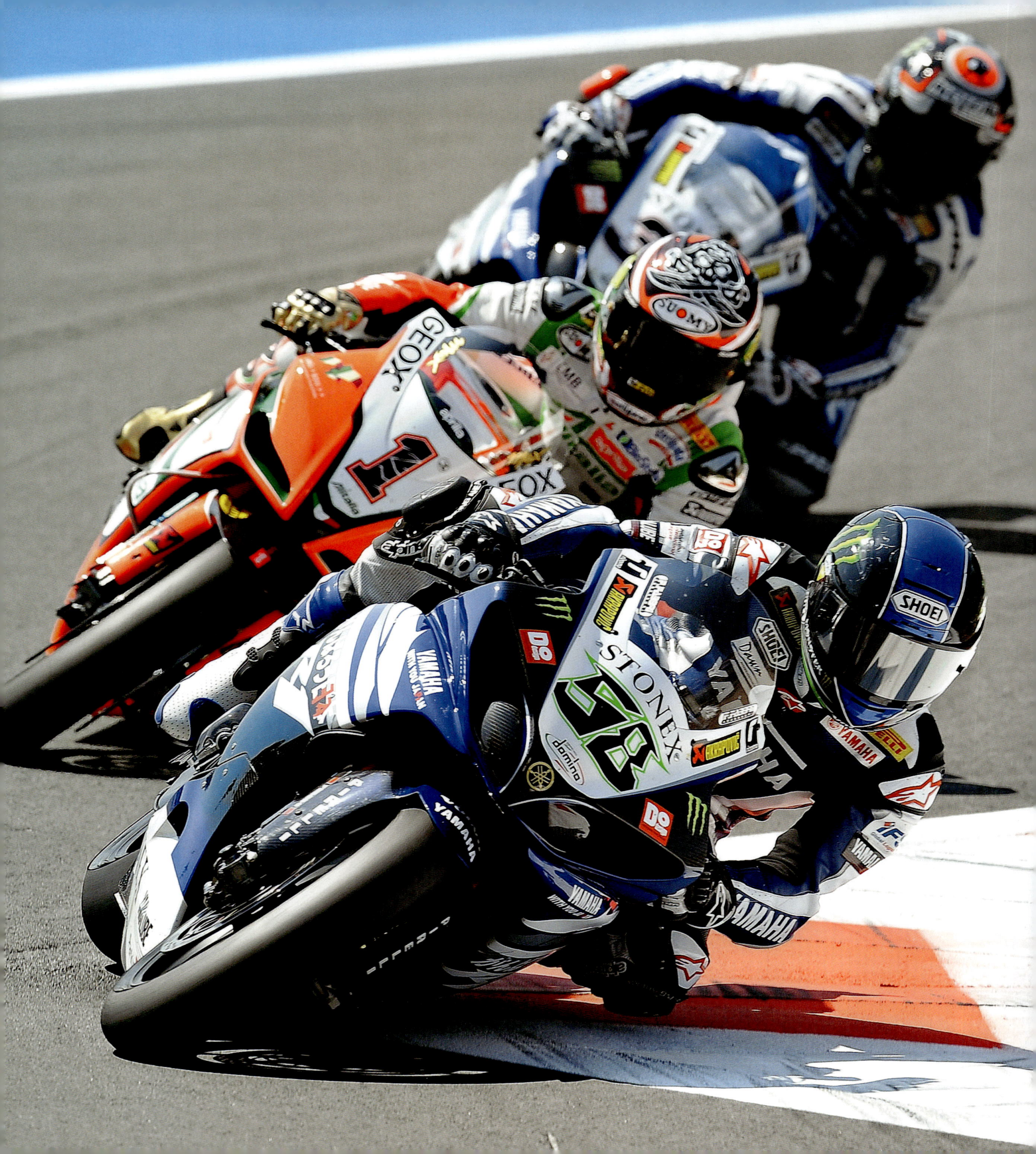
GEOX
SUOMY
SHOEI
STONEX
YAMAHA

ITALY

MONZA | 08•05

Superpole

M. Biaggi	(ITA - Aprilia)	1'41.745
		204,405 km/h

Race 1

1°	E. Laverty	(IRL - Yamaha)	31'09.584
			200,231 km/h
2°	M. Biaggi	(ITA - Aprilia)	+ 1.575
3°	L. Haslam	(GBR - BMW)	+ 3.078
4°	M. Melandri	(ITA - Yamaha)	+ 3.255
5°	M. Fabrizio	(ITA - Suzuki)	+ 11.812

Fastest lap

3°	M. Fabrizio	(ITA - Suzuki)	1'43.275
			201,377 km/h

Race 2

1°	E. Laverty	(IRL - Yamaha)	31'19.948
			199,128 km/h
2°	M. Melandri	(ITA - Yamaha)	+ 0.327
3°	M. Fabrizio	(ITA - Suzuki)	+ 2.466
4°	N. Haga	(JPN - Aprilia)	+ 2.583
5°	T. Corser	(AUS - BMW)	+ 4.502

Fastest lap

4°	M. Biaggi	(ITA - Aprilia)	1'43"023
			201,869 km/h

Many were expecting an Italian win on their home circuit, but instead Irishman Eugene Laverty (58) scored a well deserved double, beating out Max Biaggi (1) in race 1, and Marco Melandri (33) in race 2.

The favorites for the race to be contested at the fastest circuit on the World Superbike calendar were Max Biaggi and the two factory Yamaha riders. The Aprilia rider in particular was seen to have a very good chance for success, considering he scored the Superpole and double race win at the circuit in 2010.

And the Monza weekend did start well for the reigning champion, who set the fastest time in the Superpole session, averaging over 204 km/h for the lap! Max almost seemed to take flight when his Aprilia RSV4R reached a top speed of 334.8 km/h on the main straight. It was Eugene Laverty who recorded the second fastest lap, roughly six tenths off the lead pace, followed in turn by Rea and Corser, the latter rediscovering his taste for a flying lap at the Italian venue. The Ducati was suffering in terms of top speed, and Carlos Checa could manage no better than the eleventh fastest time.

Emerging to dominate the first Monza race, however, was Eugene Laverty. The 25 year old Irishman, riding in his debut Superbike season, showed no fear in the face of more experienced competition, first among them his teammate Marco Melandri. Once Laverty had taken the lead in race 1, it looked as though nobody could match his pace, not even a Max Biaggi desperate for the maximum points haul. Race 2 eventually ended with the same winning result for Laverty, although the actual course of events was quite different from race 1. The Yamaha rider actually spent the majority of the second encounter back in fourth place, until a penalty for Biaggi gave him the extra motivation to challenge Melandri for the win. An effort that paid off with the first double of his young career. Biaggi's penalty occurred when he ran long on the brakes and cut the first chicane, at which point he didn't re-enter the track according to the correct procedure as defined by Race Direction. The punishment was a ride-through, just when the Roman had built up a strong lead, dropping him back to eleventh place. He would eventually fight his way back up to eighth, but that didn't' quell the controversy that was destined to emerge after the race.

Despite failing to score a win at Monza, Marco Melandri scored a podium and enough points to put him right on Biaggi's heels in the championship standings.

Scoring his second podium of the season was BMW rider Leon Haslam, although the British rider's spirits were dampened slightly by a crash in race 2. Also crashing in the afternoon affair was Jonathan Rea (sixth in race 1), who had a disappointing weekend overall.

Michel Fabrizio recorded a satisfying third place finish in race 2 (he was fifth in race 1), showing that the Italian was finally getting to grips with his new Suzuki.

The impressive top speed of the Aprilia also

Max Biaggi was in the spotlight yet again, and once more it was because of a rules infraction. After finishing race 1 in second place, the Italian rider ran long and cut the first chicane while leading race 2, causing Race Direction to asses him a ride through penalty.

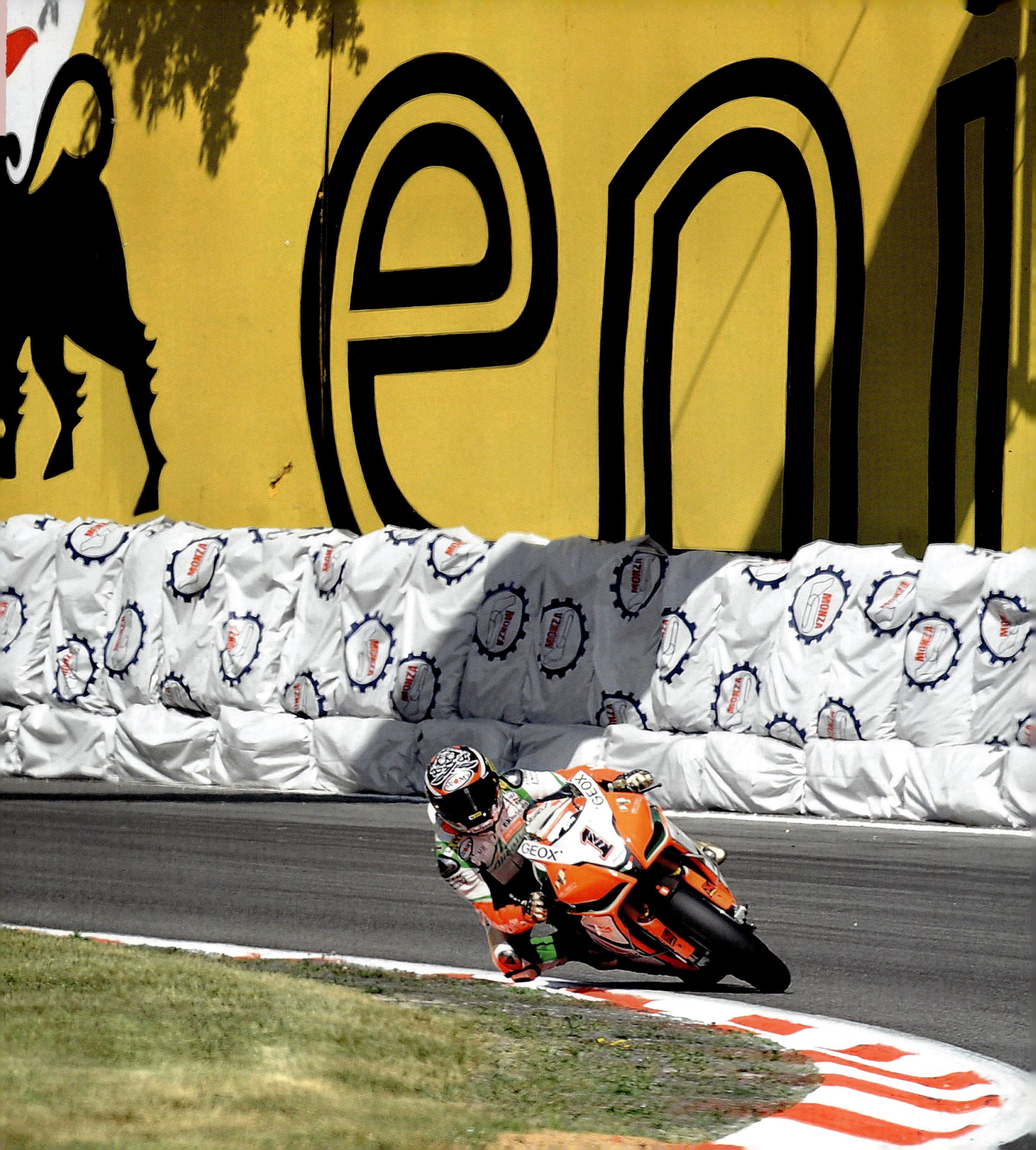
eni
MONZA
GEOX

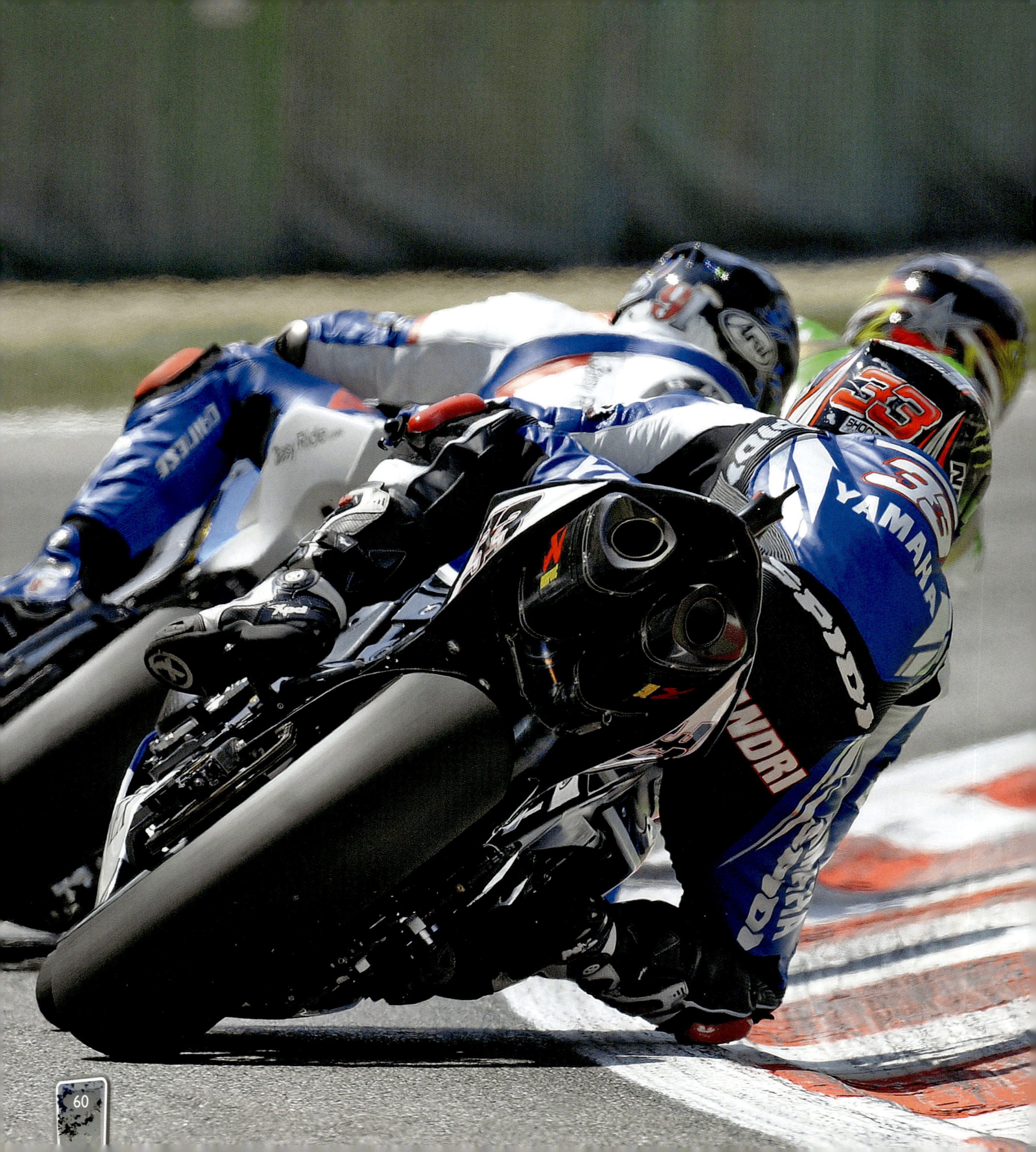
YAMAHA

WSBK RACES

helped Noriyuki Haga emerge from his early season struggles, the Japanese rider scoring a fourth place finish in race 2, after being penalized with a ride-through of his own in race 1. Championship leader Carlos Checa, severely handicapped by the speed deficit of his twin-cylinder machine, came home with ninth and tenth place finishes from the weekend, which reduced his point advantage significantly.

The Spaniard was expecting Monza to be one of the harder rounds on the calendar for his Ducati, knowing that his four-cylinder mounted rivals would enjoy a significant advantage, Max Biaggi chief among them.

Recording yet another a solid performance was Ayrton Badovini, who took home a hard fought sixth place in race 2, putting him near the top ten in championship points. Unfortunately his teammate, James Toseland, was unable to race after he unsuccessfully attempted to ride during the first free practice session.

The same fate was suffered by Chris Vermeulen, who crashed his Kawasaki during practice and was forced to sit out yet another round. Despite Monza looking like a favorable track for the Japanese manufacturer, Vermeulen's teammates also struggled for performance, with a ninth place finish the best result of the weekend for team green.

It was another quiet round for Leon Camier, the second Aprilia factory rider, who was eighth in race 1, and crashed out of race 2.

After four rounds, the championship standings see Carlos Checa leading with 145 points, followed by Marco Melandri with 118, and Max Biaggi with 117. The rest of the field is significantly further back, starting with Jonathan Rea on 89 points.

A podium and fourth place for Marco Melandri, at a track considered to be his and Yamaha's home circuit. Third place and the first podium of the year for Michel Fabrizio (84) in race 2, while that same step of the podium went to Leon Haslam (91) in race 1.

USA

MILLER | 30•05

An almost surreal climate greets the World Superibke riders and team member as they arrive at Miller Motorsports Park. It feels a lot like winter: there is a biting chill in the air, and the tops of the mountains surrounding the circuit are covered in snow. A steady rainfall during the practice sessions also contributes to the atmosphere, but luckily the sunshine would return in time for race day.

Carlos Checa had something of a score to settle with the Salt Lake City venue, the Spaniard having suffered two technical problems last year while firmly in control of both races. His good feelings with the American circuit date back to 2008, when he scored an excellent double win on the Honda.

And so it was no surprise that Checa took the Superpole, qualifying in front of another Ducati rider, Jakub Smrz, and the two Yamaha's of Marco Melandri and Eugene Laverty. Max Biaggi suffered a crash in the crucial final moments of the session, forcing him to start both races from the second row, alongside an ever improving Ayrton Badovini.

The two races were completely and thoroughly dominated by Carlos Checa, with none of his adversaries able to offer him the slightest trouble. His final gaps over the second place finishers speak for themselves, and they could have been even larger (especially in the first race) had the Spanish rider not relented in the closing laps. The only drama was created by the memories of last year's races, but this time his luck, and engines, held out, giving him a full 50 points for the weekend, further increasing his lead over Melandri and Biaggi.

Neither of the two Italians was ever a threat for the race win. Melandri spent race 1 around mid-pack, eventually finishing tenth, while he managed to get up with the front runners for the second contest, coming home sixth.

For his part, Max Biaggi crashed out along with Jonathan Rea in a fairly controversial race 1 incident, while race 2 saw him take the final step of the podium, beaten out by his teamma Leon Camier's best performance of the year.

Joining Checa on the podium for race 1 were fellow Ducati 1198 riders Jakub Smrz and Sylvain Guintoli, both from team Effenbert - Liberty Racing.

After an excellent double win for Ben Spies in 2009, the Yamaha team had high expectations for the round, but Eugene Laverty could manage only fourth and fifth place finishes.

A crash – without injury – in race 1 didn't prevent Michel Fabrizio (Suzuki) from performing admirably in race 2, the Italian the author of an exciting comeback ride that saw

Superpole
	C. Checa	(ESP - Ducati)	1'58.315
			149,307 km/h

Race 1
1°	C. Checa	(ESP - Ducati)	38'46.915
			159,425 km/h
2°	J. Smrz	(CZE - Ducati)	+ 2.766
3°	S. Guintoli	(FRA - Ducati)	+ 4.093
4°	L. Camier	(GBR - Aprilia)	+ 8.885
5°	E. Laverty	(IRL - Yamaha)	+ 15.718

Fastest lap
7°	C. Checa	(ESP - Ducati)	1'49.779
			160,916 km/h

Race 2
1°	C. Checa	(ESP - Ducati)	38'22.082
			161,145 km/h
2°	L. Camier	(GBR - Aprilia)	+ 7.194
3°	M. Biaggi	(ITA - Aprilia)	+ 8.734
4°	E. Laverty	(IRL - Yamaha)	+ 14.214
5°	M. Fabrizio	(ITA - Suzuki)	+ 14.750

Fastest lap
4°	C. Checa	(GBR - Aprilia)	1'48"827
			162,324 km/h

Fast in practice but usually inconsistent in the races, Czech rider Jakub Smrz managed to bring home a second place finish in race 1 at the picturesque Miller Motorsports Park. He finished race 2 in eighth place.

63

Among the American flags planted in the grass to remember fallen members of the military, Carlos Checa confirmed his dominance at the Salt Lake City venue. After a double win in 2008, and some poor luck in 2010, another two wins arrived this year.

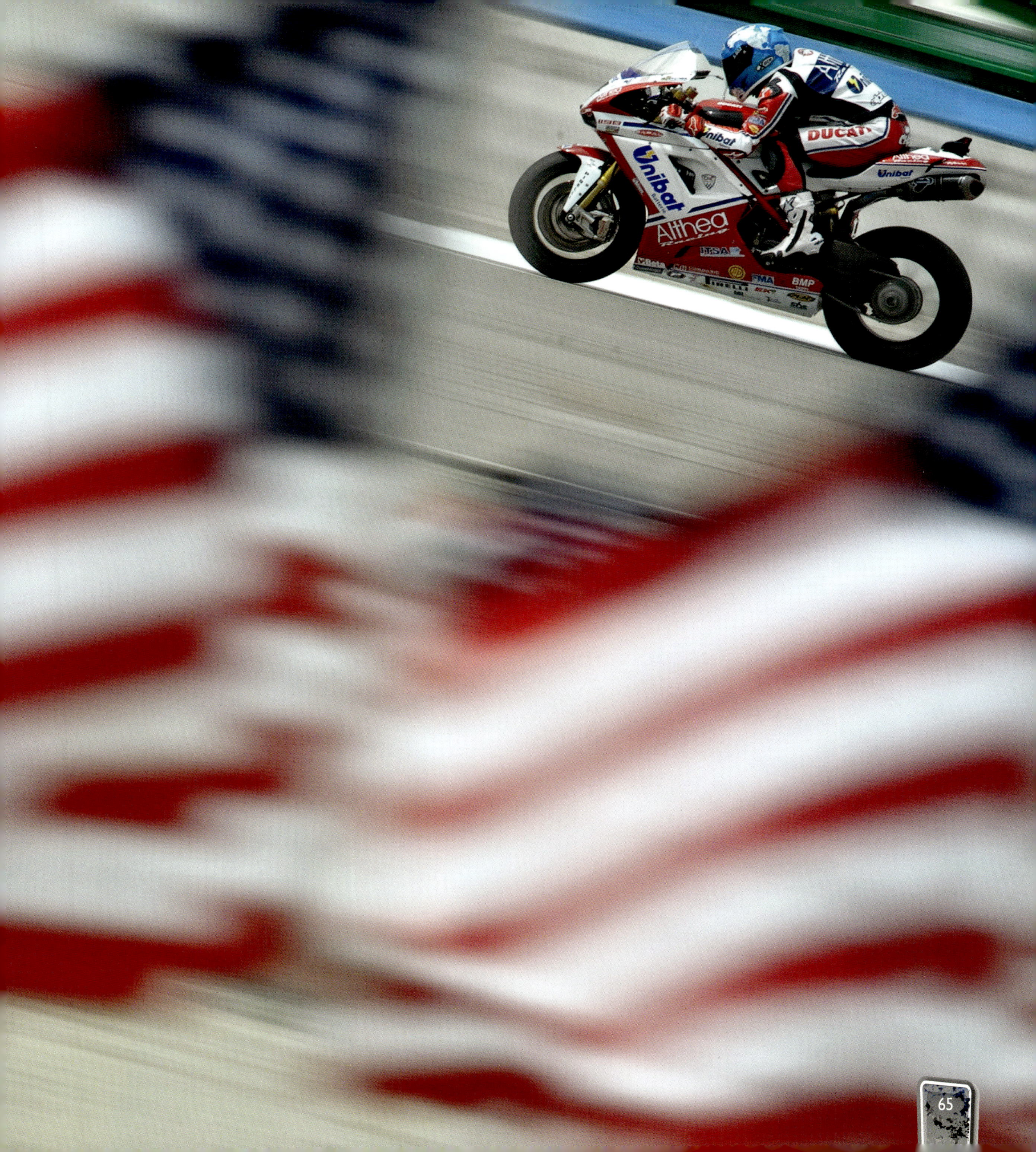
Unibat
Althea
Racing
DUCATI
ITSA
BMP
FMA
PIRELLI

66

WSBK RACES

him cross the line fifth.

Kawasaki – once again without Chris Vermeulen – only managed a sixth place finish from Tom Sykes in race 1 (Lascorz never broke the top ten), while the factory BMW squad was even further behind (Haslam eighth and thirteenth). Troy Corser started race 1 in fine form, but a trip through the gravel relegated him to the back of the field, where he eventually finished thirteenth, and a crash at the start of race 2 completely halted the Australian's progress on that occasion.

Performing slightly better was Ayrton Badovini on the satellite BMW, who bested Haslam in a race 1 duel, and was the top S 1000 RR rider in race 2 (ninth). Attempting yet another comeback – following a testing crash at Motorland Aragon – was James Toseland, but the pain in his arm kept him from starting race 2, at which point he and the BMW Motorrad Italia team decided he should have further medical tests performed before he would ride again.

Another big disappointment was the Castrol Honda team, which saw Spaniard Ruben Xaus crash out of both races, while Jonathan Rea, who also hit the ground in race 1, could manage nothing more than eleventh place in the day's second contest.

A curious incident took place at the conclusion of race 1, when Carlos Checa actually managed to crash after taking the checkered flag (due to an excess of enthusiasm…), forcing the Ducati rider to hitch a ride back to the pit lane with Toseland, in order to participate in the podium ceremony. In any case, he didn't seem overly worried about standing on the top step with his leathers covered in mud.

Following the Miller round, the championship standings saw Carlos Checa increase his lead to more than sixty points over Melandri and Biaggi. Even greater was the gap to the group riders behind them, consisting of Eugene Laverty, Leon Haslam, Jonathan Rea and Leon Camier, in that order.

Max Biaggi (top left on the podium with Checa) managed only a third place finish in America, behind his teammate Leon Camier (2). Checa asked Toseland for a ride back to pit lane, since he had crashed after crossing the finish line in race 1. Narrowly missing the podium in both races was Eugene Laverty (58).

X-lite
X-802
SINCE 1973
ITSA
Unibat
Batterie
Althea
DUCATI
1198
7
PIRELLI
BMP
TAPPI
Beta
FMA

SAN MARINO

MISANO | 12•06

Superpole
T. Sykes	(GBR - Kawasaki)	1'55"197
		132,066 km/h

Race 1
1°	C. Checa	(ESP - Ducati)	39'03.132
			155,828 km/h
2°	M. Biaggi	(ITA - Aprilia)	+ 0.984
3°	M. Melandri	(ITA - Yamaha)	+ 17.124
4°	T. Sykes	(GBR - Kawasaki)	+ 18.652
5°	E. Laverty	(IRL - Yamaha)	+ 18.929

Fastest lap
5°	C. Checa	(ESP - Ducati)	1'36.660
			157,393 km/h

Race 2
1°	C. Checa	(ESP - Ducati)	22'44.117
			156,138 km/h
2°	M. Biaggi	(ITA - Aprilia)	+ 1.484
3°	N. Haga	(JPN - Aprilia)	+ 7.772
4°	A. Badovini	(ITA - BMW)	+ 7.856
5°	L. Haslam	(GBR - BMW)	+ 9.714

Fastest lap
3°	C. Checa	(ESP - Ducati)	1'36.520
			157,621 km/h

It was the third double win of the season for Carlos Checa (Ducati), who beat out Max Biaggi (Aprilia) in both races. The Spnaiard thus increased his championship lead, while Biaggi moved up to second place in the points standings.

A rain shower disturbed the Superpole session, bringing the wet weather specialists to the fore. First among them was Tom Sykes, who scored his second Superpole with Kawasaki after doing the honors at Imola in 2010, also on a damp track. Qualifying behind the British rider was Carlos Checa, who continues to perform well, even on those tracks which theoretically don't favor the Ducati. Joining them on the front row were Jakub Smrz (Ducati) and Marco Melandri (Yamaha), while an engine problem forced Max Biaggi and his Aprilia onto row two. The Italian rider was also dealing with small injury to his left ankle, suffered in a free practice crash.

The San Marino round lost another of its protagonists in the morning warm up session: Jonathan Rea (Honda) was the victim of a crash as spectacular as it was violent, which broke his right radius bone and left him with no possibility to race.

Carlos Checa scored yet another double win (his third of the season), getting the best of Max Biaggi in both races despite an honest effort from the Aprilia rider to stop the Spaniard's winning streak. The 2010 World Champion actually held the lead for more than half of race 1, up until the point where Checa made the decisive pass. Max did his best to resist, but there was little he could do against the Ducati rider's superior pace. Checa and Biaggi were destined to battle again in both parts of race 2, the afternoon contest interrupted by a red flag for an incident involving Melandri and Camier.

The Aprilia rider ceded the win to his Ducati counterpart yet again, but his pair of second place finishes were enough to overtake Marco Melandri in the championship points standings. The Yamaha rider did manage a podium in race 1, despite a significant gap to the leaders, but the aforementioned crash kept him out of the points in race 2.

Taking that final podium place in the afternoon race was Noriyuki Haga (Aprilia), who had suffered a technical problem with his bike in race 1.

Tom Sykes (Kawasaki) showed that his dry weather pace was also quite competitive, taking his ZX-10R to fourth place in race 1, and fourteenth place in race 2, even though he actually crashed and was forced to rejoin from last place. His teammate Joan Lascorz showed some progress as well, coming home with a pair of ninth place finishes.

A regular feature among the front runners this season, Irishman Eugene Laverty managed a fifth place result in race 1, before crashing in race 2 and winding up thirteenth. Overall it was a weekend that didn't meet his expectations.

Just missing out on a race 2 podium was

70

MOTUL
SUZUKI
VIRU
PHLOGAS
Beta

Unibat
Batterie
Althea
alpinestars
GEOX
PIRELLI
1198

WSBK RACES

We saw the first podoium of the season for Noriyuki Haga (Aprilia), above, while a race 2 crash prevented Marco Melandri from repeating his third place result from race 1. It was another impressive performance for Ayrton Badovini (86), who narrowly missed out on the podium in race 2, after an exciting battle with Haga and Haslam.

BMW rider Ayrton Badovini. After an eighth place result in the morning race, the Italian was involved in an exciting duel with Haga and Haslam for third place, but the Japanese rider eventually won out. Staying with the Italian BMW squad, there was noteworthy performance from Lorenzo Lanzi, who was called in to ride James Toseland's S 1000 RR. The Italian scored points in both contests, which is a solid result considering that the bike was completely new to him before the weekend started.

Leon Haslam gave the impression that he could put his factory BMW up amongst the front runners, mixing it up with Biaggi and Checa early on in race 2. The red flag seemed to interrupt his rhythm, however, and he wound up fighting for a distant third place, eventually finishing fifth. A banged up Troy Corser only started the first race, and then pulled in after just five laps, putting an early end to his day.

Two seventh place finishes were the tally for Sylvain Guintoli, the Frenchman proving to be the second fastest Ducati rider of the day, behind only Checa. Crashing out of both contests, however, was his teammate Jakub Smrz, and these performances only served to highlight the excellent job Carlos has done to maximize the Ducati package this season. Beyond the Czech team, the other Ducati on the grid is ridden by young Frenchman Maxime Berger.

At the conclusion of the Misano round, the championship standings saw Checa continue to lead (245 points), followed now by Biaggi (173), Melandri (150), Laverty (123) and Haslam (106).

YAMAHA
YAMAHA
FACTORY RACING
SPIDI
YAMAHA
YAMAHA
YAMALUBE

BOMBOOGIE
DELLORTO
BMW
X-lite
SPYKE
BMW Motorrad Italia

ARAGON | 19•06

The World Superbike championship made its way to the brand new Motorland Aragon Circuit for the first time, one of the most impressive venues on the series calendar. The production based bikes used a slightly different track layout than their MotoGP counterparts, and it featured an uphill section at the end of the long straightaway which the riders cited as being particularly challenging.

It was Marco Melandri who took the first Superpole at the track, and the first of his WSBK career, making the most of Max Biaggi's draft to beat the Aprilia rider by 156/1000 in the end. Also performing well on the Italian machine was Leon Camier, who filled out the front row along with Carlos Checa.

The most important incident of the entire weekend came on lap eight of the first race, when Carlos Checa went down while trying to keep pace with leaders Melandri and Biaggi. The gap in top speed performance was evident, but the championship leader attempted to defy expectations once again, this time with less positive results.

Carlos chose a more prudent approach in race 2, finishing in third place, even if the gap to winner Biaggi was almost seven seconds. The result allowed the team Althea Racing rider to maintain a healthy championship points lead over his nearest competitors. The net loss to Biaggi was 29 points for the round, however, and this could possibly have been a hit to the Ducati rider's morale.

Max Biaggi, knowing that the Spanish round was crucial to his championship, decided to go on the attack, and partook in excellent battles with Melandri during both races. In the first contest he led for fifteen of the twenty laps, up until a mistake (he ran long) allowed Marco to take the lead and open a small gap. In race 2, however, the reigning world champion left no room for his competitors, beating his Yamaha mounted compatriot across the finish line by five seconds.

The fight with Biaggi – an old rival of his – seemed to provide extra motivation for Melandri, who was going all out for the double win after taking the first contest. It was his mistake, however, that eventually allowed the Roman to break away and win. In any case, the former 250cc world champion is the only rider, along with Max, who still has a chance of troubling Checa for the title.

His teammate, Eugene Laverty, was never a threat for the win at Aragon, as was the case with Biaggi's teammate Leon Camier, who was third in race 1 and eighth in race 2.

Superpole

	M. Melandri	(ITA - Yamaha)	1'57.634
			163,545 km/h

Race 1

1°	M. Melandri	(ITA - Yamaha)	40'01.968
			160,189 km/h
2°	M. Biaggi	(ITA - Aprilia)	+ 1.572
3°	L. Camier	(GBR - Aprilia)	+ 2.432
4°	E. Laverty	(IRL - Yamaha)	+ 10.799
5°	T. Sykes	(GBR - Kawasaki)	+ 10.847

Fastest lap

7°	C. Checa	(ESP - Ducati)	1'58.862
			161,855 km/h

Race 2

1°	M. Biaggi	(ITA - Aprilia)	40'04.407
			160,026 km/h
2°	M. Melandri	(ITA - Yamaha)	+ 4.809
3°	C. Checa	(ESP - Ducati)	+ 6.944
4°	M. Fabrizio	(ITA - Suzuki)	+ 9.001
5°	J. Lascorz	(ESP - Kawasaki)	+ 11.562

Fastest lap

3°	M. Melandri	(ITA - Yamaha)	1'59.159
			161,452 km/h

The weekend could have been a triumphant homecoming for Carlos Checa, who nearly ruined the party with a crash in race 1. This mistake allowed Biaggi and Melandri to take a sizable bite out of his championship lead.

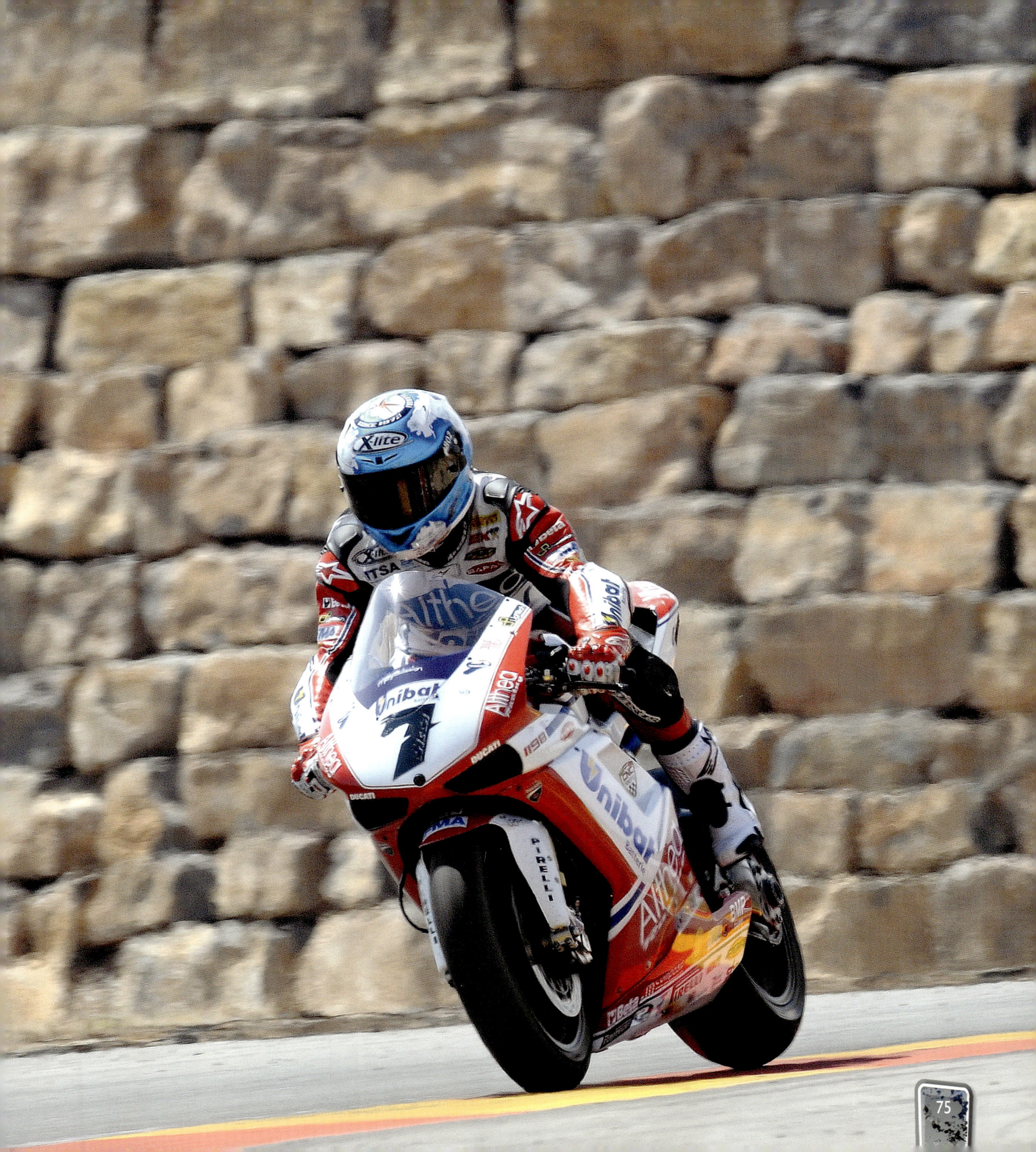
X-lite
Althea
Unibat
7
PIRELLI

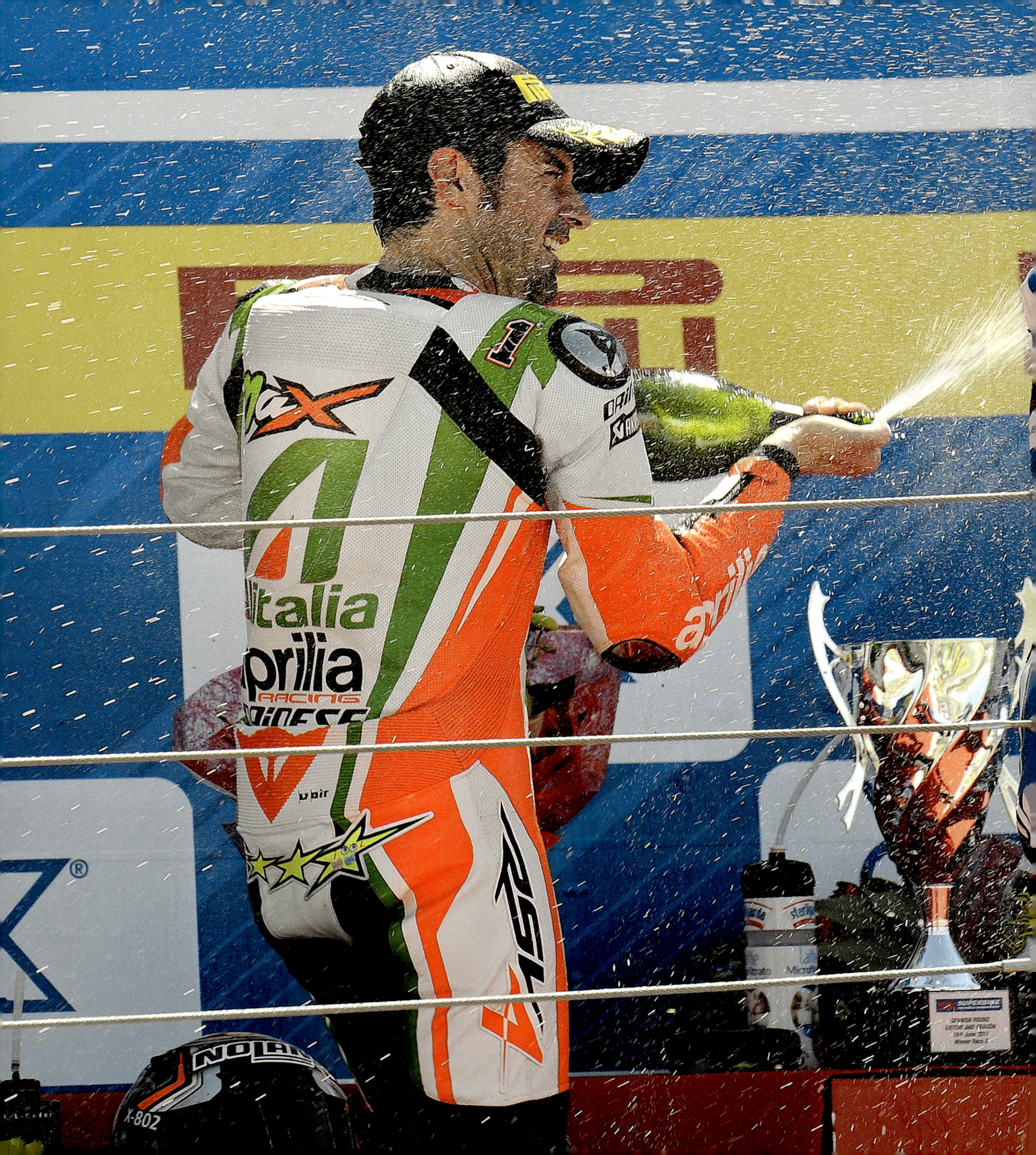
aprilia
RACING
NOLAN
X-802

Max Biaggi and Marco Melandri exchanged race wins, giving both valuable points and allowing them both to make the most of Checa's mistake. For Max it was his first victory of the season.

PIRELLI
SHOEI
SPIDI
eni
aprilia
Alitalia
3
SBK
TISSOT
SUPERPOLE
Aragon
17, 18, 19 June 2011
SBK SUPERBIKE

WSBK RACES

Kawasaki continued to improve its dry weather performance – even if still far from the leaders – with two fifth place results, one form Tom Sykes and one from Joan Lascorz. Also showing good pace was Michel Fabrizio, the lone Suzuki rider on track, who rebounded from a race 1 crash to take fourth place in the second race, thus conserving his seventh spot in the championship standings.

An honest result was also tallied by Noiyuki Haga on the team PATA Racing Aprilia, with sixth and seventh place finishes in the round that saw his 300th career race in World Superbike.

Ayrton Badovini again beat out his factory BMW colleagues in race 1, finishing eighth ahead of Haslam and Corser. Speaking of the British rider, Leon reached a milestone of his own during the weekend, notching up his 100th presence in WSBK.

Absent from the race, aside from Jonathan Rea who was injured at Misano, was James Toseland, again replaced by Lorenzo Lanzi.

Competing in both Aragon races was Chris Vermeulen, the Australian putting in maximum effort, even if the results were still well below his expectations. Also far from the front runners was Ruben Xaus, bringing up the rear on the only Honda present during the weekend.

Following the Aragon round, Carlos Checa has 261 points, against 218 for Biaggi, and 195 for Melandri. These new totals keep the championship fight alive, while further behind are Laverty (146), Camier (125), Haslam (120) and Michel Fabrizio (108).

Race 1 saw the third podium of the year for Leon Camier (2) on the factory Aprilia, while the British rider finished race 2 in eighth. Michel Fabrizio (84, pictured ahead of Ayrton Badovini) came back from a race 1 crash to finish just off the podium in the second contest.

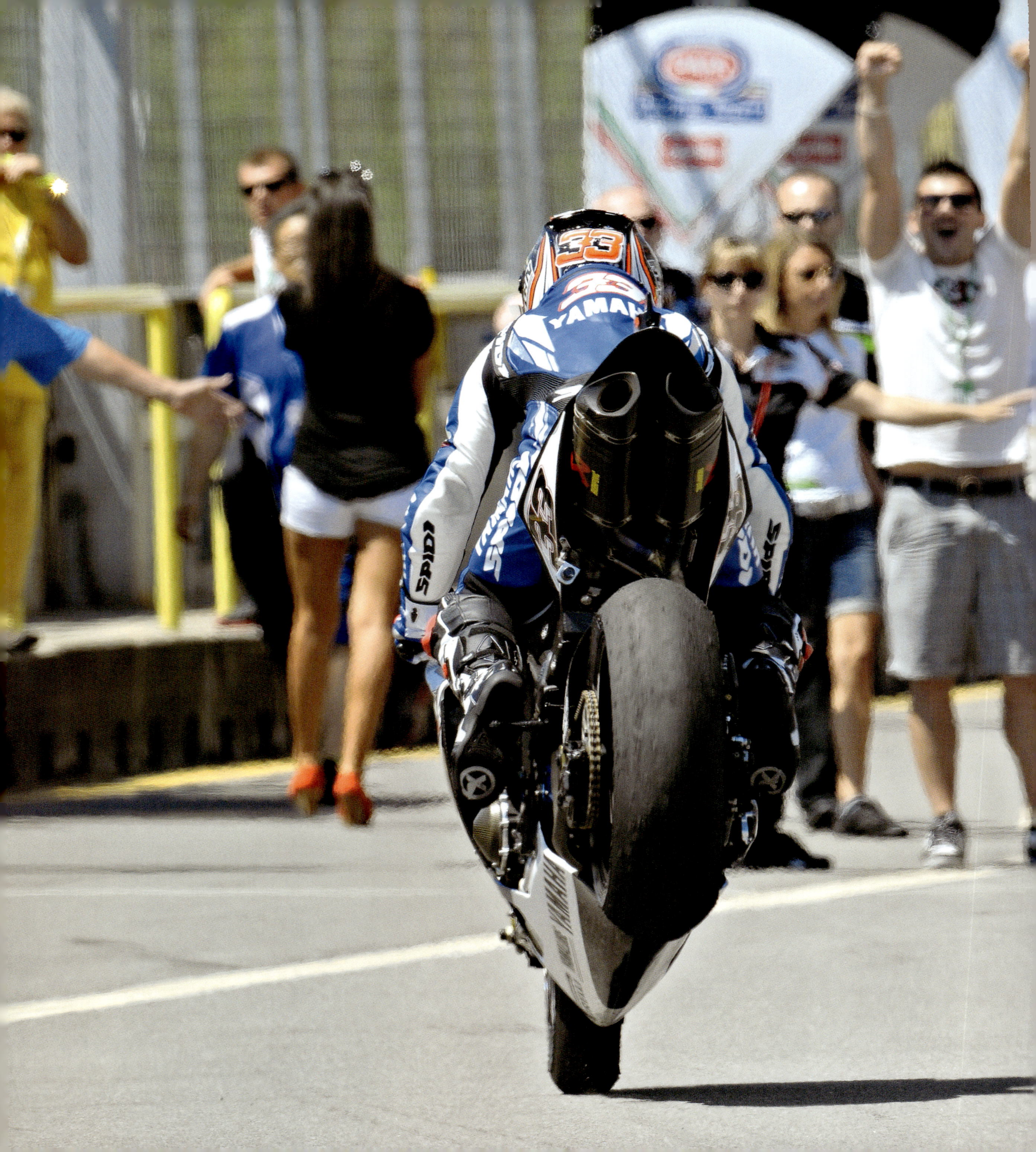
33
SPIDI

BRNO

AUTOMOTODROM BRNO | 10•07

Superpole		
M. Biaggi	(ITA - Aprilia)	1'58.580
		164,031 km/h

Race 1			
1°	M. Melandri	(ITA - Yamaha)	40'23.699
			160,505 km/h
2°	M. Biaggi	(ITA - Aprilia)	+ 0.241
3°	C. Checa	(ESP - Ducati)	+ 0.436
4°	M. Fabrizio	(ITA - Suzuki)	+ 8.448
5°	E. Laverty	(IRL - Yamaha)	+ 11.863

Fastest lap			
3°	M. Melandri	(ITA - Yamaha)	2'00.118
			161,931 km/h

Race 2			
1°	M. Biaggi	(ITA - Aprilia)	40'21.546
			160,641 km/h
2°	M. Melandri	(ITA - Yamaha)	+ 0.222
3°	C. Checa	(ESP - Ducati)	+ 3.558
4°	M. Fabrizio	(ITA - Suzuki)	+ 7.863
5°	E. Laverty	(IRL - Yamaha)	+ 8.534

Fastest lap			
2°	M. Melandri	(ITA - Yamaha)	2'00.058
			162,012 km/h

Marco Melandri celebrates his impressive race 1 win at Brno. The Yamaha rider finished the day with a second place finish in race 2, behind the same Max Biaggi that he beat in the first contest.

There was Czech Republic round was highly anticipated after Carlos Checa's misadventures in Spain. Indeed, Brno is one of Max Biaggi's favorite circuits, and the Italian has always enjoyed strong races there. This meant that the Aprilia rider had an excellent opportunity to further cut into the Spaniard's already shrinking championship lead.

In an effort to land an early psychological blow, Biaggi took the Superpole on Saturday, beating out Marco Melandri by two tenths, and Checa by three.

Missing from the starting grid were Troy Corser (who underwent surgery following his Aragon crash), and Jonathan Rea, replaced this time by British rider Alex Lowes. James Toseland once agian attempted to ride his BMW, but after the first practice session he ceded the controls to Lorenzo Lanzi once more.

As expected based on the practice results, race 1 saw a tight battle between Marco Melandri (Yamaha) and Max Biaggi (Aprilia). The two Italians held nothing back, and once Checa lost contact with them at half race distance, their duel only intensified as they each pushed the gain the most points possible. In the end it was Melandri who came out on top, denying Biaggi the satisfaction of another Brno win.

The Aprilia rider didn't have to wait very long for his revenge, leading for most of race 2 and rebuffing the attacks of Melandri, who actually passed him for the lead on two occasions. The reigning world champions was not to be denied, however, and he took control when it mattered most, crossing the finish line first.

Checa, realizing that there was little he could do at the Czech circuit, decided to protect this third place spot in race 1, taking the same position uncontested in race 2.

Michel Fabrizio has always performed well at Brno, and the Alstare Suzuki rider took home a pair of fourth place finishes on the weekend. He managed to edge out Eugene Laverty on both occasions, the Irishman holding onto fourth in championship points thanks to Leon Haslam's less than brilliant performance.

Two sixth place finishes were the reward for an excellent effort from Ayrton Badovini, who was the top BMW rider in both races. The result allowed the young Italian to take eighth place in the championship standings, an honorable result considering it was his team's first year competing in World Superbike. And beyond the actual results, Badovini's race was also positive thanks to the aggressive riding he displayed.

Leon Haslam, riding the only factory BMW in action, wound up with seventh and eighth place finishes, enough to gain one spot in the

The Brno round was characterized (just like Aragon) by a double battle between Max Biaggi (1) and Marco Melandri (33), which ended in another draw. Trying to mix it up with them in race 1 was Carlos Checa (7), who had to settle for a pair of third place finishes.

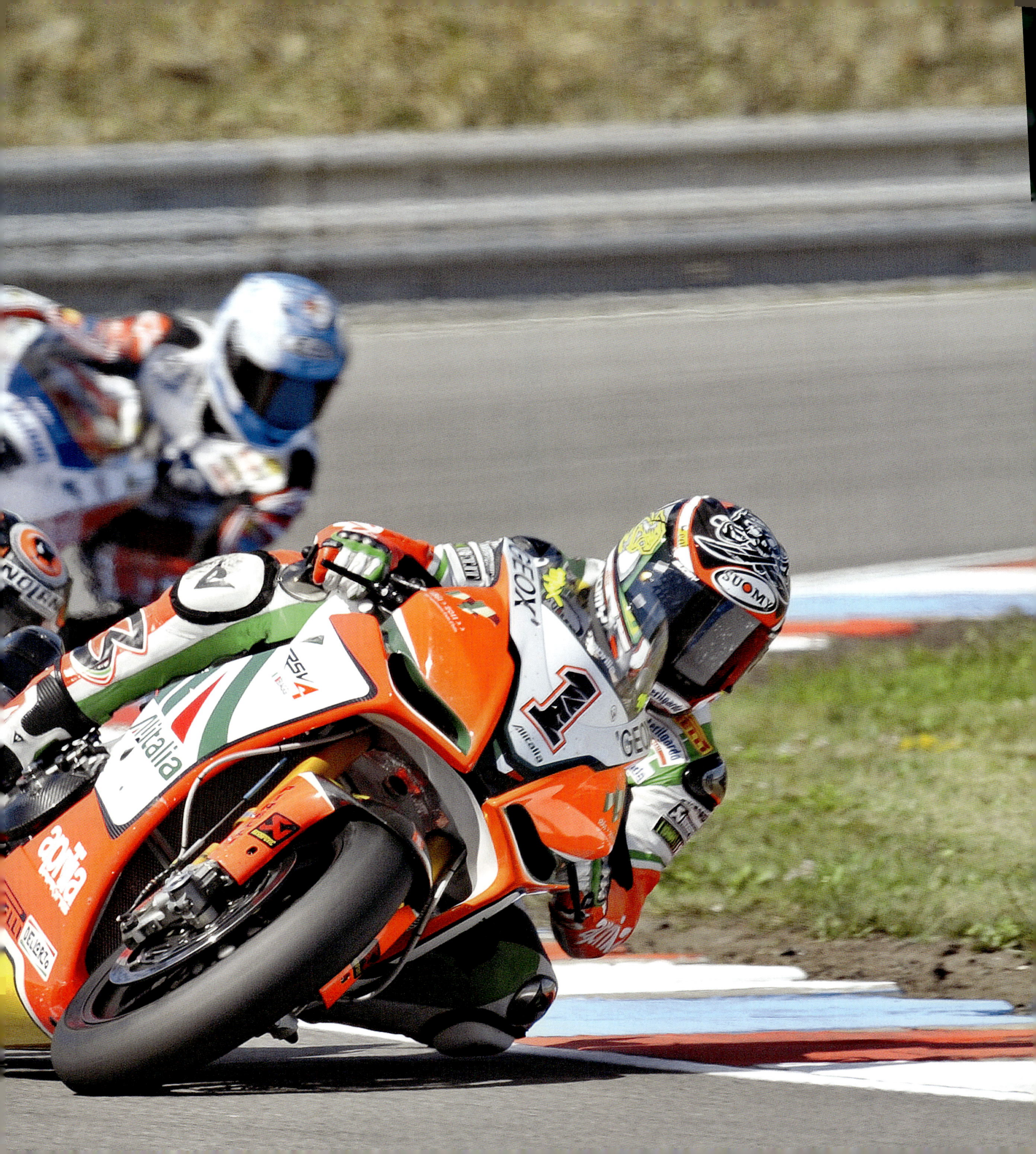
SUOMY
GEOX
RSV4
Alitalia
aprilia

WSBK RACES

The Brno circuit is on of Max Biaggi's favorites, and he reminded everyone by scoring the Superpole. Despite a committed effort, Carlos Checa (7) wasn't able to trouble the two race winners. Ayrton Badovini (86) took home two important sixth place results in the Czech Republic.

standings at the expense of Leon Camier (Apriia), who crashed in race 2.

Kawasaki was still far from the front runners, and this time the top finishing ZX-10R was that of Joan Lascorz, the Spaniard taking home an eight and a ninth place finish. Speaking of the Ninja (which is the name the Japanese bike goes by), the improved performance of team Pedercini was worth pointing out, their bikes ridden by Mark Aitchison and Roberto Rolfo.

Not much was expected of substitute rider Alex Lowes, but the Briton nevertheless performed well on the only Castrol Honda at Brno. The twenty year old scored points in race 1, and unfortunately crashed out of the second contest.

Racing in front of their home crowd didn't provide much help to team Effembert - Liberty Racing, and their riders Smrz and Guintoli. The former crashed out of yet another race, while the Frenchman suffered a technical problem in race 1, and finished just ninth in race 2.

Speaking again about the injured riders, there was the umpteenth attempt by Chris Vermeulen to return to normal action, but the Australian was forced to stop for the day after race 1. Ruben Xaus was involved in a spectacular and violent crash on the first lap of the first race, putting an end to his day as well.

The championship standings after the Czech round see Checa still leading (293 points) with a diminished gap to Max Biaggi, now just 30 points behind. Also gaining ground was Marco Melandri (240), while the best of the rest were Laverty on 168 points, and Haslam on 137.

85

SILVERSTONE

SILVERSTONE | 31•07

The riders and teams of the World Superbike series arrived to find a Sivlerstone Circuit that was recently renovated and improved.

On paper the historic venue was expected to be difficult for Carlos Checa and his Ducati, so their preparation for the race were meticulous.

Providing a lot of curiosity was the presence of John Hopkins. The Anglo-American is considered one of the fastest riders in the world, and has already made some appearances in WSBK aboard a Honda. This time he is competing as a wild card, riding the Suzuki he regularly races in BSB.

And "Hopper" – this is his long time nickname – immediately showed what all the hype was about, taking the Superpole from Eugene Laverty by 27/1000. The home track advantage also proved useful to Leon Camier, the Aprilia rider setting the third quickest time, just ahead of Carlos Checa. Max Biaggi failed to advance past the second knockout phase, and was forced to start the race from row three.

Carlos Checa dominated race 1, giving Ducati their 300th win in World Superibke. The Spaniard understood that the British round was fundamental, and chose to go on the attack, beating early race leader Eugene Laverty by over three seconds in the end. Checa managed a repeat performance in race 2, with Laverty again leading the opening laps before the Ducati rider caught and passed him for the win. The two wins helped to boost Checa's championship points lead back up to a healthy margin, over sixty points more than his nearest rival.

Yamah again proved the competitiveness of their package, allowing Laverty and Melandri to finish second and third, respectively, in both races. The Irishman even led portions of each race, but eventually had to give way to an extremely strong Checa. Melandris strong performances also allowed him to gain ground on Max Biaggi in the championship standings.

Max was hindered in race 1 by contact with Troy Corser at the start, which damaged one of his clip-ons and forced him to do some… acrobatic riding just to finish eleventh. Race 2 saw Biaggi partake in an exciting battle with Melandri, which the Yamaha rider only barely won at the finish line. The Italian pair both got around Leon Camier late in the race, relegating the British rider to fifth place.

Completing the top five in race 1 was John Hopkins, the Suzuki rider having staying with the lead group throughout the contest, running as high as third at one point. His second race went much the same way, even if he eventually finished down in seventh place. Riding the other Suzuki (that of team Alstare) Michel Fabrizio came home ninth in race 2, after having crashed on lap one of the first race.

Superpole
	J. Hopkins	(USA - Suzuki)	2'04.041
			171,292 km/h

Race 1
1°	C. Checa	(ESP - Ducati)	38'06.477
			167,266 km/h
2°	E. Laverty	(IRL - Yamaha)	+ 3.304
3°	M. Melandri	(ITA - Yamaha)	+ 4.782
4°	L. Haslam	(GBR - BMW)	+ 7.116
5°	J. Hopkins	(USA - Suzuki)	+ 11.057

Fastest lap
5°	C. Checa	(ESP - Ducati)	2'06.045
			168, 568 km/h

Race 2
1°	C. Checa	(ESP - Ducati)	38'03.361
			167,494 km/h
2°	E. Laverty	(IRL - Yamaha)	+ 2.274
3°	M. Melandri	(ITA - Yamaha)	+ 3.675
4°	M. Biaggi	(ITA - Aprilia)	+ 3.960
5°	L. Camier	(GBR - Aprilia)	+ 4.405

Fastest lap
2°	M. Biaggi	(ITA - Aprilia)	2'05.525
			169,267 km/h

Flying beneath the Silverstone podium was a flag celebrating Ducati's 300th victory in World Superbike. The excellent early season win tally of Carlos Checa helped them reach the milestone even faster.

87

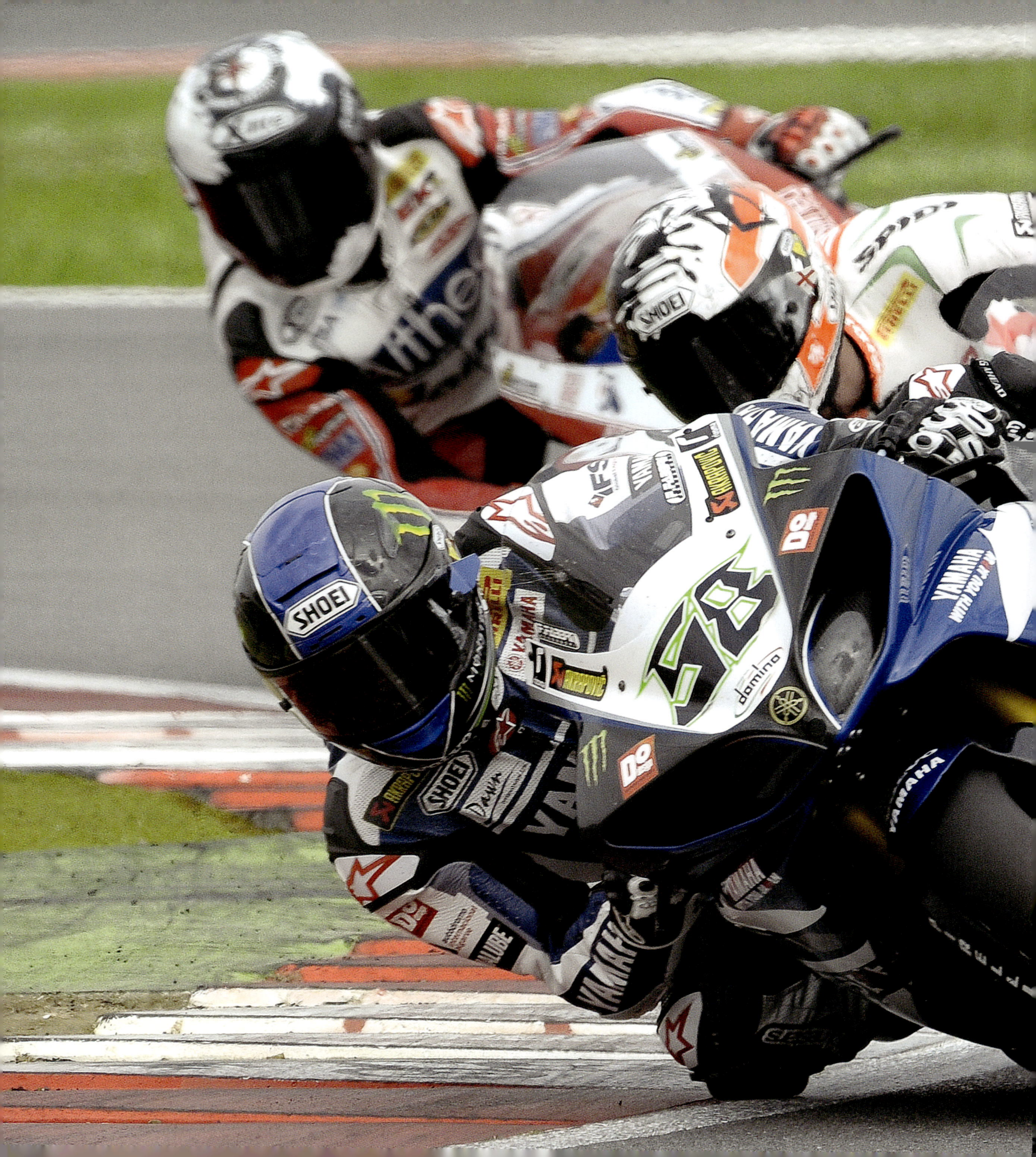
SHOEI
78
domino
YAMAHA
SPIDI

Eugene Laverty (58) scored a pair of second place finishes, the Irishman beating out teammate Marco Melandri on both occasions. For his part, Leon Camier (2) managed one fifth place finish at home.

Another double win for Carlos Checa, pictured here with engineer Ernesto Marinelli, head of the Superbike program at Ducati Corse. The maximum points haul allowed the Spaniard to increase his championship lead.

WSBK RACES

Leon Haslam (BMW) also ran among the leaders in race 1, taking down fourth place in the end. Unfortunately he couldn't reproduce the performance in race 2, where he finished eighth.
Less inspiring was the performance of Haslam's BMW teammate Troy Corser, while James Toseland managed to complete both races, albeit far from the top riders. A pair of tenth place finishes allowed Ayrton Badovini to keep his tenth place spot in the standings.
Frenchman Sylvain Guintoli left the British round with a further twenty points on his tally, thanks to a couple of sixth place finishes on his Ducati. Suffering another lackluster weekend was Kawasaki, the Japanese manufacturer doing without Tom Sykes, who injured himself in free practice. This left them pinning their hopes on Joan Lascorz, who finished seventh in race 1, but concluded race 2 empty handed due to a technical problem.
It was an unlucky second WSBK appearance for Alex Lowes on the Castrol Honda. The British rider crashed out of one race and retired from the other because of a bike problem, giving the highly regarded Ten Kate team one of their worst results of the season.
A crash and a retirement also characterized Noriyuki Haga's Silverstone round, leaving the Japanese rider at the margins of the top ten in points, an usual position for the heralded Superbike veteran.
At this stage in the season, the championship standings see Carlos Checa (343 points) with a 62 point advantage over Max Biaggi (281), and a 71 point lead on Marco Melandri (272). Laverty gained some ground on those immediately in front of him, but he was still well behind the Spaniard (- 135).

There were high expectations for John Hopkins, who partially delivered on them by taking Superpole on the Samsung Crescent Suzuki. Max Biaggi didn't fare so well in qualifying, winding up on the third row.

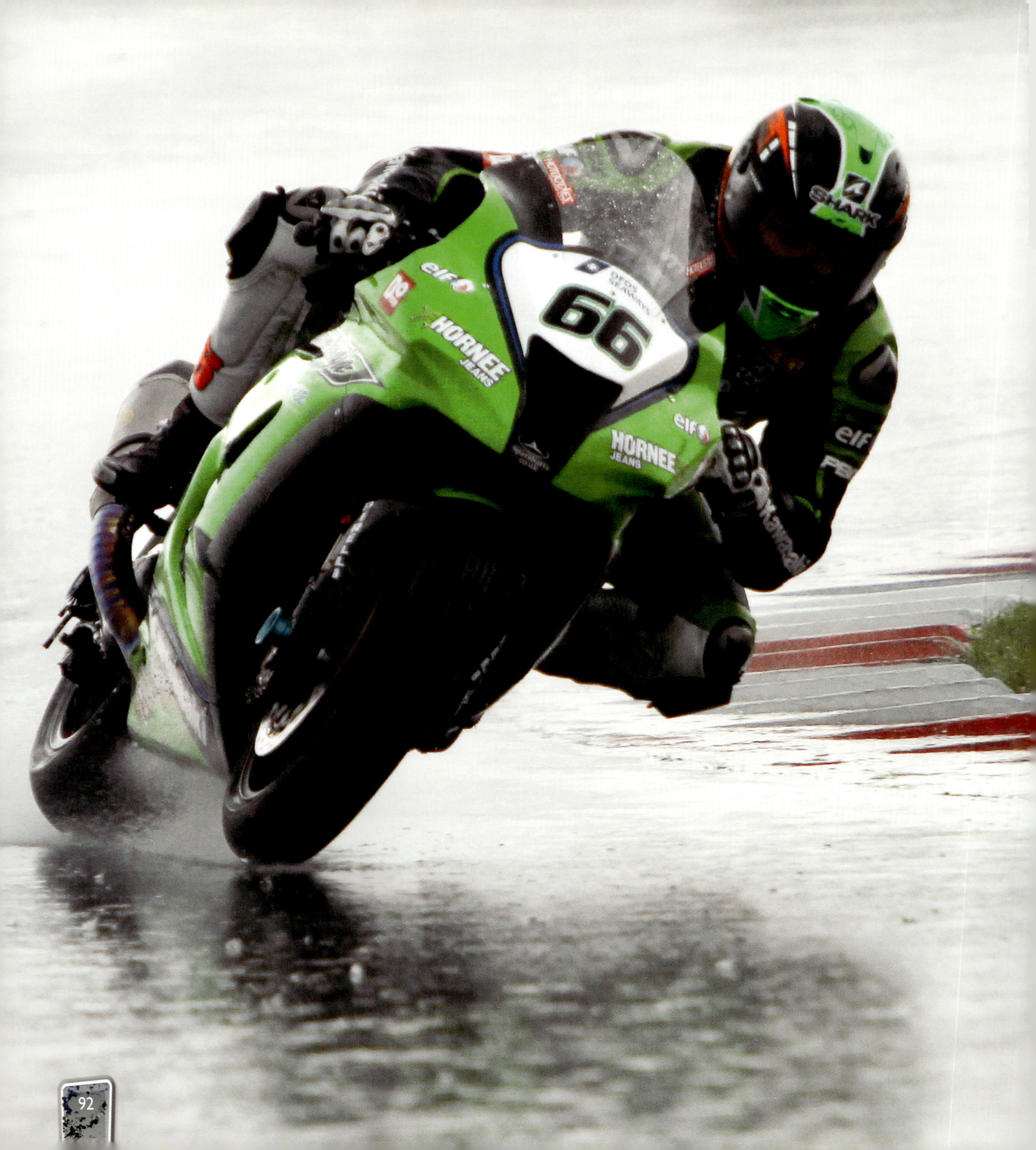
SHARK
elf
DFDS SEAWAYS
66
HORNEE JEANS
elf
HORNEE JEANS
elf

NÜRBURGRING

NÜRBURGRING PARK | 27•03

Superpole		
C. Checa	(ESP - Ducati)	1'54"144
		162,016 km/h

Race 1			
1°	C. Checa	(ESP - Ducati)	38'59"779
			158,076
2°	M. Melandri	(ITA - Yamaha)	+ 1.855
3°	N. Haga	(JPN - Aprilia)	+ 2.322
4°	E. Laverty	(IRL - Yamaha)	+ 7.789
5°	L. Haslam	(GBR - BMW)	+ 9.727

Fastest lap			
4°	C. Checa	(ESP - Ducati)	1'55"971
			159,464 km/h

Race 2			
1°	T. Sykes	(GBR - Kawasaki)	29'49"337
			134,358 km/h
2°	S. Guintoli	(FRA - Ducati)	+ 4.063
3°	J. Smrz	(CZE - Ducati)	+ 22.759
4°	J. Rea	(GBR - Honda)	+ 28.497
5°	E. Laverty	(IRL - Yamaha)	+ 38.374

Fastest lap			
7°	N. Haga	(JPN - Aprilia)	2'14"619
			137,374 km/h

An image that gives some idea of the race 2 conditions, where Tom Sykes triumphed on his Kawasaki. The contest was actually halted when the minimum race distance was reached, at which point Race Direction decided to show the red flag.

The German round was the first event following the shock announcement that the official Yamaha team was pulling out of World Superbike. It was a hard blow for the series, considering that the Japanese manufacturer had been a constant presence in the paddock for many years.

The second shock came during the second free practice session, when Max Biaggi was hit in the foot by a sewer grate, leaving him with a serious fracture that kept him out of the races. This essentially put an end to the Aprilia rider's hopes of catching Carlos Checa in the championship standings, and in turn left the Spaniard free to concentrate fully on Marco Melandri, his only real competition remaining. Prior to the German round, Biaggi was trailing Checa by 62 points (with 200 still to play for), while Melandri had a gap of 71 to the leader.

Returning to action, meanwhile, was Jonathan Rea. The Honda rider was fully recovered from the injury he suffered at Misano, and had also just signed a new contract with the Japanese manufacturer for 2012.

Carlos Checa (Ducati) was not distracted by anything going on around him, and not only did he take the Superpole, he broke the existing track record that belonged to Max Biaggi (Aprilia). The Italian rider actually managed to compete in Superpole, and it was only after the session that his fractured foot was fully diagnosed. He had qualified third in the process, just behind the Yamaha of Eugene Laverty, and in front of that of Marco Melandri.

It goes without saying that race 1 was a breakaway win for Carlos Checa, who took the lead on lap three and continued to build his advantage from there. At one point his lead was as large as four seconds, but he eventually crossed the line with gap to Marco Melandri of a little under two seconds.

Heavy rain wreaked havoc with race 2, which saw Checa take an extremely cautious approach, careful not to make any big mistakes. The Spaniard eventually finished eighth, which was a decent result considering that his nearest title challenger Melandri was sixth.

At a circuit where he has always gone well, Noriyuki Haga was up amongst the leaders in both races. In the first contest he actually led for a few laps, and eventually settled in to a battle with the Yamaha riders, taking the third step of the podium. In the second race he stormed out to the lead in the wet conditions, looking dominant – his advantage was over nine seconds! – right up until the moment when he crashed and threw away a likely win.

Marco Melandri rode aggressively in race 1, finishing as the runner up, but he took a more cautious approach in the heavy rainfall that characterized the afternoon affair. Meanwhile, his teammate Eugene Laverty, who had battled

41
PATA
Unibat
Althea
alpinestars
DUCATI
PIRELLI

SUPER
PIRELLI
DAINESE
Kawasaki
Kawasaki

SHOEI
Red Bull
Castrol
4
HONDA

DAINESE
DAINESE
Castrol
Ride

SBK MILESTONE ACHIEVEMENT
JAMES TOSELAND
200 Races
in the Superbike World Championship
Nürburgring - Race 1
Sunday 4 September 2011

WSBK RACES

Second place for Sylvain Guintoli (50, Ducati) who actually pressured Sykes for several laps. Returning to the front was Noriyuki Haga (41) who unfortunately crashed while leading race 2. Also scoring podiums were Jakub Smrz (96) and Marco Melandri (33), the Italian finishing second in race 1.

with Marco in race 1, concentrated on staying upright in race 2, gaining valuable points in his effort to catch Max Biaggi in the standings.

The flood-like conditions of the second race (it was really and truly pouring down) understandably brought the wet weather specialists to the fore. First among them was Tom Sykes, who scored his first World Superbike win with a four second gap to second placed Sylvain Guintoli (Ducati). The result was crucial to the British rider's effort to sign another contract with Kawasaki for 2012, or even find another open seat.

Adding to the strong performance for team Effenbert - Liberty Racing was the third place finish of Jakub Smrz, who managed a podium while being some twenty seconds behind the race winner. It is worth noting that Guintoli may have had the speed to challenge Sykes, but he preferred to protect his second place finish.

Ayrton Badovini performed well yet again on the satellite BMW, while his factory team colleague Leon Haslam went even better with a fifth place finish in race 1. Not as impressive was Troy Corser, with Makoto Tamada equally disappointing in his substitute ride for Ruben Xaus. James Toseland suffered a crash in race 2, and was subsequently taken to the circuit Medical Center. A few days later the British rider announced his immediate retirement from racing, the right hand injuries suffered at Motorland Aragon preventing him from ever riding again at the top level.

After the hectic and controversial German round, Carlos Checa's points total grew to 376, compared to 302 for Melandri, who overtook the stationary Biaggi (281) for second place in the standings. The Aprilia rider was also starting to feel pressure from Eugene Laverty, who improved to 232 points.

96

97

ITALY

IMOLA | 25•09

A medical exam confirmed that Max Biaggi would not be fit to race in the Imola World Superbike round. This forfeiture definitively ended the Roman's chance of defending his crown, no matter how slim it might have been.

Speaking of things coming to an end, the unfortunate retirement of James Toseland forced the BMW Italia team to call in Javier Fores, who races a German four-cylinder in the Spanish national championship, as a last minute replacement.

A motivated and fairly relaxed Carlos Checa was able to edge out Jonathan Rea by just 78/1000 for the Superpole. There were some surprises, however, as Noriyuki Haga (Aprilia) and Tom Sykes (Kawasaki) unexpectedly qualified third and fourth fastest, respectively.

A scary moment came when Carlos Checa crashed in the morning warm up session, but luckily he was uninjured.

The adoption of a new ride by wire system finally allowed Honda to fight on equal terms with their Superbike competition, and Jonathan Rea made the most of it, leading nearly all of race 1 once he got past the quick starting Sykes. Not that Rea's race was all smooth sailing from there, as Noriyuki Haga eventually caught up to him, and then did everything in his power to try and get past for the lead. The Honda rider was not to be denied, however, and he responded to Haga's attacks blow for blow, eventually winning out by a slim margin.

The Imola round could have seen an impressive double win for Rea, but his Honda let him down with a technical problem in race 2. Meanwhile, Carlos Checa seemed to be approaching the day's races in two distinct ways. In the first – thinking about the championship standings – he simply focused on the third step of the podium, probably realizing that he could match the pace and intensity being shown by Rea and Haga. In the second, after seeing how Marco Melandri was struggling, he decided to throw caution to the wind and race the way he likes most. From half race distance he began a comeback charge that quickly saw him on Rea's tail, eventually inheriting the race lead when the British rider pulled out. From that point on the Spaniard's pace was impossible for anyone to match, including Haga who finished over four seconds behind.

A sixth place result for Marco Melandri prevented Checa from mathematically clinching the title, but the three points he needed seemed easily obtainable in the four races (two rounds) remaining in the championship. Melandri never looked comfortable at the Imola circuit (which was practically unknown to him), and in race 1 he finished down in eighth place.

Superpole

	C. Checa	(ESP - Ducati)	1'47"196
			165,767 km/h

Race 1

1°	J. Rea	(GBR - Honda)	38'03"396
			163,424 km/h
2°	N. Haga	(JPN - Aprilia)	+ 0.111
3°	C. Checa	(ESP - Ducati)	+ 9.449
4°	T. Sykes	(GBR - Kawasaki)	+ 9.792
5°	E. Laverty	(IRL - Yamaha)	+ 14.699

Fastest lap

12°	C. Checa	(ESP - Ducati)	1'47"960
			164,594 km/h

Race 2

1°	C. Checa	(ESP - Ducati)	38'04"538
			163,342 km/h
2°	N. Haga	(JPN - Aprilia)	+ 4.631
3°	L. Camier	(GBR - Aprilia)	+ 15.159
4°	E. Laverty	(IRL - Yamaha)	+ 17.195
5°	L. Haslam	(GBR - BMW)	+ 17.288

Fastest lap

13°	C. Checa	(ESP - Ducati)	1'47"934
			164,634 km/h

After an entertaining battle with Noriyuki Haga, Jonathan Rea (4) took the race 1 victory, thanks in part to the new ride by wire system that rejuvenated his Castrol Honda.

Red Bull
www.jonathan-rea.com
Arai
Castrol
Ten Kate
Honda Racing
HONDA
4

100

The forced absence of Max Biaggi didn't quel Carlos Checa's (7) will to win, getting into duels with Eugene Laverty (58) and Noriyuki Haga (41) along the way. Earlier the Spaniard had scored a third place finish in race 1. The two results put Checa just three points shy of the World Championship title, delaying the celebrations till the next round.

SHOEI
SPIDI
aprilia
2
Alitalia
RSV4
CAMIER
PIRELLI
1861 > 2011 >
AKRAPOVIC

WSBK RACES

Noriyuki Haga seems to have plenty of fans in Italy, and they were treated to the sight of two aggressive races from the Japanese rider, who narrowly missed out on a win at the circuit where he last triumphed in 2009.

It also appears as though Tom Sykes really enjoys the Italian venue, where last year he achieved his first career Superpole, and this season he took fourth place in race 1. Unfortunately he couldn't repeat the performance in race 2, as he was forced to retire with a technical problem.

Other Ducati riders scoring top ten results included Sylvain Guintoli (and Jakub Smrz in race 1), while wild cards Federico Sandi and Alessandro Polita both scored points on the twin-cylinder machines.

Not so impressive this time around was Ayrton Badovini (his best result was ninth in the first race) whom many expected more from in his home race. Doing a little better was fellow BMW rider Leon Haslam, who finished fifth in race 2, after having crashed out of race 1.

Another highlight was the strong round from Australian Mark Aitchison on the team Pedercini Kawasaki, who finished both races just behind factory rider Joan Lascorz. Instead it was a weekend to forget for Michel Fabrizio (Suzuki) who crashed in the first race and was forced to retire from the second.

As mentioned, just three points separated Carlos Checa from the championship title, while Melandri looked ever more secure in second place, thanks in part to Max Biaggi's forced stop. Eugene Laverty continued to gain ground on the Roman, who was just 25 points ahead at that point.

The honor of being top Aprilia rider fell Noriyuki Haga at Imola. The Japanese racer (41) took home two second place finishes, barely missing out on the win in one of them. Factory Aprilia rider Leon Camier (2) finished on the podium in race 2.

MAGNY COURS 20
SUPERBIKE
2011 WORLD CHAMPION
Althea Racing
Althea Racing
PIRELLI
FIM
the FIRST "TORO"
SUPERBIKE 2011
WORLD CHAMPION
2011

FRANCE

MAGNY-COURS | 02•10

Superpole

J. Rea	(GBR - Honda)	1'37"490
		162,884 km/h

Race 1

1°	C. Checa	(ESP - Ducati)	38'16"465
			159,040 km/h
2°	M. Melandri	(ITA - Yamaha)	+ 2.201
3°	L. Haslam	(GBR - BMW)	+ 3.218
4°	L. Camier	(GBR - Aprilia)	+ 3.796
5°	E. Laverty	(IRL - Yamaha)	+ 5.602

Fastest lap

4°	C. Checa	(ESP - Ducati)	1'38"643
			160,981 km/h

Race 2

1°	C. Checa	(ESP - Ducati)	38'17"851
			158,945 km/h
2°	M. Melandri	(ITA - Yamaha)	+ 1.267
3°	E. Laverty	(IRL - Yamaha)	+ 2.043
4°	L. Haslam	(GBR - BMW)	+ 6.506
5°	S. Guintoli	(FRA - Ducati)	+ 7.843

Fastest lap

2°	C. Checa	(ESP - Ducati)	1'39"136
			160,180 km/h

Carlos Checa triumphantly raised the trophy that gave him the title of 2011 World Superbike Champion.
The Spaniard didn't want to sit back and count points, instead taking a double win in France.

Carlos Checa needed only three points – from either one of two races – to win the 2011 World Superbike Championship. Riders and teams are always extremely cautious, and even superstitious, but the final result was all but assured.

Superpole saw another top performance from Jonathan Rea, who truly returned to competitiveness with the adoption of ride by wire on his Honda. The British rider set a new track record, beating out Laverty, Checa and Camier in the process.

All eyes were focused on Carlos Checa for race 1, and the Spaniard didn't merely settle for the necessary three points. Instead he chose to demonstrate how he obtained such a big lead in the first place, by adding to his string of victories (and double wins). So after Eugene Laverty had led the first several laps of the race, the Ducati took command and proceeded to win by more than two seconds over Marco Melandri, his closest competitor in the title race.

Race 2 was conducted in a slightly different way, with the Spaniard running in fourth place until around half race distance, at which point he began his unstoppable charge toward the front. The end result was Checa's fifth double win of the season, which not only awarded him the Riders' Championship, but also secured the Constructors' title for Ducati.

Unlucky in race 2 was Jonathan Rea who, following a race 1 crash, spent a significant number of laps in first and second place before his Honda let him down with a technical issue.

Taking home two second place finishes was Marco Melandri, the protagonist of two splendid comeback rides after a pair of lackluster starts. In race 1 he battled with Haslam, Camier and Laverty, who finished behind him in that order, while the second contest saw him again find added speed in the latter stages, once more getting the best of his Yamaha teammate Laverty. For his part, the Irishman featured heavily in both races, but also began to fade later on each time.

Magny Cours saw Leon Haslam again looking competitive on the BMW, landing on the podium in the first race, and just missing it in the second. Overshadowed by this was his teammate Troy Corser, who had already announced he would retire from racing at the end of the season, in order to concentrate on testing for the German marque: a way of staying on the scene without the added commitment of racing.

Absent once again was Max Biaggi, still suffereing from his Nurburgring injury, leaving Leon Camier as the lone factory Aprilia rider. The Englishman finished just off the podium in race 1, and followed it up with sixth place in race 2.

While Carlos Checa was the undisputed star of the show, you couldn't forget the supporting cast of Marco Melandri (33), Leon Haslam (91) and Leon Camier (2), who all raced at the front.

CARLOS CHECA GALLARDO
SINCE 1972
X-lite
X-802
ITSA
Unibat
Batterie
Althea
Racing
DUCATI
1198
PIRELLI
FMA
maya design
Beta
alpinestars

PIRELLI
SHARK
GRAZIE
SIDI
Liberty
Media

YAMAHA
WITH YOU JAPAN

Althea

WSBK RACES

And it was still superior to what Noryuki Haga could manage on the team PATA Aprilia.

Mixing it up with the front runners was home rider Sylvain Guintoli, who continued the streak of good form that began with the Silverstone round and the Nurburgring podium. Meanwhile his teammate Jakub Smrz suffered his umpteenth crash during race 1, and didn't take the start of race 2.

And speaking of crashes, Michel Fabrizio managed to notch up two of them, as the Italian was having a particularly difficult end to his season.

Not particularly impressive in France were the Kawasakis, with a best result of seventh place in race 2, while a struggling Tom Sykes crashed out of that same contest.

Also going down twice in Friday practice was Ruben Xaus, which resulted in the doctors pulling his clearance to race. He would also miss the next round at Portimao, bringing an early end to a very difficult season for the Spaniard. Xaus, one of the most spectacular riders in the series, nevertheless stated his intention to return for the 2012 season.

Ayrton Badovini – again paired with Javier Fores in place of Toseland – was another rider who left Magny Cours on a less than positive note. His eighth place finish in race 2 allowing him to stay in the top ten in points, however.

By this point the World Championship had come to a close, with Carlos Checa winning the title over Marco Melandri, who had in turn clinched second place. Still up for grabs was third in points, with Eugene Laverty (283 points) just pulling ahead of Max Biaggi (281), who was expected to return to action at Portimao.

Another good performance from Sylvain Guintoli (top left) who was often among the front runners in the latter stages of the season. There were mixed feelings at Yamaha, with the retirement of the official team weighing on the podiums for Melandri and Laverty.

PORTUGAL

PORTIMÃO | 16•10

As is often the case, there was little to be sad about during the final round of the 2011 season, as most people in the paddock were already looking ahead to next year. In fact, a test session was scheduled for the Tuesday following the race, during which time we would get our first glimpse of 2012.

Returning to action, although still not fully fit, was Max Biaggi, who wanted to be present at the Portuguese circuit as his title was handed over to Carlos Checa. The Roman's weekend got off to a poor start, however, when he was eliminated from the first round of Superpole, forcing him to start both races from the fifth row on Sunday.

Taking down the Superpole was Jonathan Rea (Honda), who edged out the Ducati of Carlos Checa, and the two Yamahas of Eugene Laverty and Marco Melandri.

And it was a Ducati which led for more than half of race 1, but it wasn't the world championship winning team Althea machine, rather it was a team Eeffenbert - Liberty Racing bike, with Sylvain Guintoli at the controls. The Frenchman was looking nearly unstoppable until Checa found another gear and started a furious comeback, which at times looked hopeless since Guintoli clearly had every intention of holding the lead. With just three laps remaining Checa's pressure finally paid off, the Spaniard getting in front and staying there for his fifteenth race win of the season, which speaks volumes about how thoroughly dominant he was.

Satisfied with his race 1 conquest, Checa spent all of race 2 in fourth place, leaving the final win of the season to Marco Melandri.

Sylvain Guintoli's weekend was completed with a fifth place finish in race 2, which put him sixth in championship points for 2011.

Race 2 was completely dominated by Yamaha, as first Eugene Laverty, and then Marco Melandri, led the field. The Italian, motivated by his new contract with BMW for 2012, wanted to end the year with a win, and thus brought his total to four victories in his maiden World Superbike season.

Jonathan Rea was surely shooting for the win after taking Superpole, but the race pace of his competitors was just too strong, forcing him to settle for a pair of respectable third place finishes.

Max Biaggi's return to racing, after a month and a half of inactivity, was fairing convincing, but as Biaggi himself pointed out, the lack of fitness training adversely affected his results, which were fourth and seventh place finishes. This was enough, however, for the Aprilia rider to regain third in the championship standings.

The top Kawasaki rider at Portimao was Joan Lascorz, who scored a fifth place finish, while Tom Sykes looked less convincing than usual, actually pulling out early from race 2.

Superpole
	J. Rea	(GBR - Honda)	1'41"712
			162,529 km/h

Race 1
1°	C. Checa	(ESP - Ducati)	38'13"293
			158,587 km/h
2°	S. Guintoli	(FRA - Ducati)	+ 2.860
3°	J. Rea	(GBR - Honda)	+ 8.481
4°	M. Biaggi	(ITA - Aprilia)	+ 11.963
5°	J. Lascorz	(ESP - Kawasaki)	+ 13.333

Fastest lap
3°	S. Guintoli	(FRA - Ducati)	1'43"453
			159,794 km/h

Race 2
1°	M. Melandri	(ITA - Yamaha)	38'11"326
			158,723 km/h
2°	E. Laverty	(IRL - Yamaha)	+ 1.075
3°	J. Rea	(GBR - Honda)	+ 1.363
4°	C. Checa	(ESP - Ducati)	+ 2.648
5°	S. Guintoli	(FRA - Ducati)	+ 3.355

Fastest lap
2°	J. Lascorz	(ESP - Kawasaki)	1'43"553
			159,640 km/h

Marco Melandri finished the 2011 season with an excellent win at the Portuguese circuit, beating his teammate Laverty after an intense battle. The Portimao round was the last for the official Yamaha World Superbike team.

PORTUGUESE ROU
PORTIMÃO 2011
SBK
SUPERBIKE
FIM WO ONSHIP
YAMAHA
PIRELL
PIRE
Po imão

Once again Carlo Checa did not want spend a weekend without a win, and at Portimao he also celebrating his championship title on Sunday night in a local hotel, surrounded by riders, team members, and local authorities.

113

He tried his best to take the win from Marco Melandri, but Eugene Laverty (58) was forced to settle for second place in race 2. The result put him even on points with Max Biaggi, but third place went to the Italian. Another good race for Sylvain Guintoli, who finished on the podium in race 1.

WSBK RACES

Maxime Berger's last race of the season, and last race with team Supersonic, gave him the extra motivation to keep up with the other Ducati riders, finishing with a well deserved seventh place.

With his mind already on next year – when he will receive and thoroughly updated bike – Leon Haslam put in a mid-table performance, still managing to finish fifth in championship points during his first season on the four-cylinder German machine. And speaking of things coming to an end, the Portuguese round saw veteran rider Troy Corser's career conclude after a most impressive 377 races.

Returning to World Superbike after a long absence was Karl Muggeridge, the Australian filling in for the injured Ruben Xaus on the team Ten Kate Honda.

Also scoring points on the weekend was Michel Fabrizio, but it wasn't enough for the Roman to stay in the top ten in points. He concluded the season in twelfth place.

Managing that feat, however, was his compatriot Ayrton Badovini, who finished his second full Superbike season (and first with BMW) exactly tenth in points, an important result for both the young rider and his team. Another young Italian, Davide Giugliano, made his Superbike debut at Magny Cours, after winning the FIM Cup Superstock 2011 championship. The opportunity was a reward from Ducati, who provided him with a bike by way of the team Althea garage.

Also noteworthy was the participation of team Yoshimura-Suzuki with Josh Waters doing the riding. It was his first ever visit to the Portuguese circuit, and thus he did well to finish both races, albeit far from the leaders.

Two podiums were the final tally for Jonathan Rea in Portugal. Without his injury at Misano, the British rider would have concluded the championship much higher than ninth in the standings. Troy Corser celebrated the final race of his career, together with his colleagues and friends.

115

WSBK TEAMS

MiTo
Alfa Romeo
MiTo
Althea
Unibat
Althea
PATA
YAMAHA
Kawasaki Racing Team
ÖHLINS

WSBK TEAMS

ALTHEA Racing

An effort in the true spirit of the World Superbike Championship, which gives every team the chance to compete for victory.

Thanks to a substantial financial investment, the team from Civita Castellana has developed a professional atmosphere, and assembled a group of technicians that can ensure a high level of competitiveness with the 1198, the bike that Carlos Checa used to win the 2011 world title.

An impressive 14 races were won by Althea's single rider operation, with whom some members of the team started their adventure back in World Supersport, before moving up to Superbike. This valuable experience has allowed them to keep up with the Ducati technicians who joined them for this season from the disbanded factory team.

Carlos Checa (at left) was born on October 15, 1972, in Barcelona. The Ducati 1198 is in its fourth season of World Superbike competition, and won the 2008 Championship with Troy Bayliss.

APRILIA Alitalia Racing Team

The 2010 World Championship winning team definitely achieved less than they had planned for (and deserved); their two victories with Max Biaggi paling in comparison to the ten they achieved in the previous season.

The team's second rider, Leon Camier, was slightly disappointing as well, with just four podium finishes on the year.

After a long series of victories and titles won with two-stroke motorcycles, Aprilia returned to Superbike - they were last present almost a decade ago - with a highly technological motorcycle, which won the title in only its second year of competition.

Max Biaggi, the 2010 World Superbike Champion, was born in Rome, on June 26th, 1971. Leon Camier was born in Ashford, on August 4th, 1986. The Aprilia RSV4R was presented in late 2008, and made its WSBK debut in 2009, winning a race in its first season, at Brno.

The Italian team gained experience with the S 1000 RR in FIM Cup Superstock, continuing their progression this season with the Superbike version. Ayrton Badovini (at right) was born in Biella on May 31st, 1986, while James Toseland (below) was born on October 5th, 1980, in Sheffield.

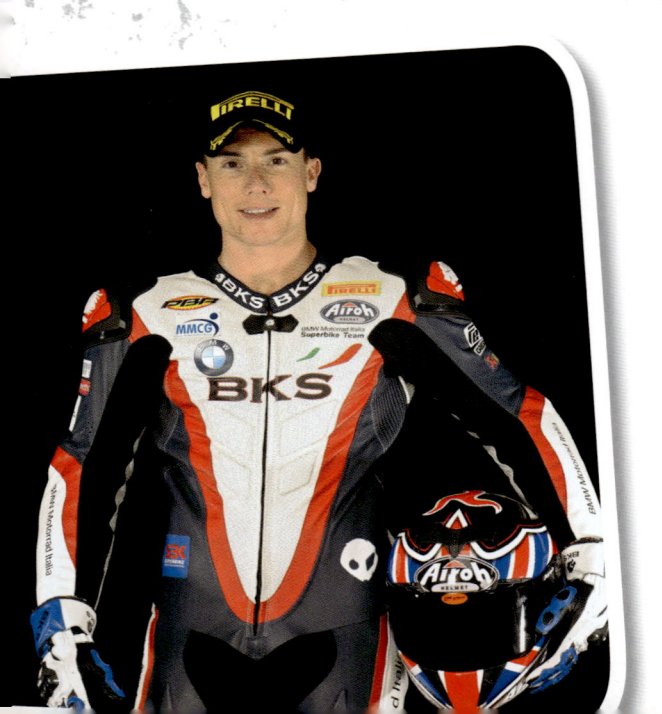

BMW Motorrad Italia SBK Team

A young team - this is their first year of participation in World Superbike, after several seasons in Superstock 1000 - which still boasts a long history. In fact, the backbone of the team is comprised of experienced members who have achieved considerable success with other marques. The combination of Italian team and German manufacturer provided surprisingly strong results, despite the forced retirement of James Toseland in the middle of the season.

Ayrton Badovini, winner of the 2010 FIM Superstock Cup with the same team and also riding a S1000RR, benefitted by receiving most of the squad's attention, and used this help to frequently outperform the factory BMW team riders. These strong results allowed the Italian to finish the season in the top ten in points.

BMW Motorrad Motorsport

One of the biggest motorcycle manufacturers in the world, the German marque decided to enter World Superbike in 2009, to make their return to racing at the international level. They still haven't achieved a race win, but their riders have secured numerous podium finishes in one of the most competitive series in the world. The considerable efforts made by BMW, since the start of their program, have been largely focused on developing the technology already present on the S1000RR road bike. The team's work methods have always been based on the philosophies of the German manufacturer, and then applied over numerous winter test sessions. As they continued to rely on the experience of Australian rider Troy Corser to help develop the new machine, this season he was paired with one of the fastest riders on the grid, 2010 championship runner-up Leon Haslam.

The S 1000 RR is one of the best selling motorcycles in the hypersport market segment. Leon Haslam (above) was born in Derby, on May 31st, 1983. Troy Corser was born on the 27th of November, 1971, in Wollongong.

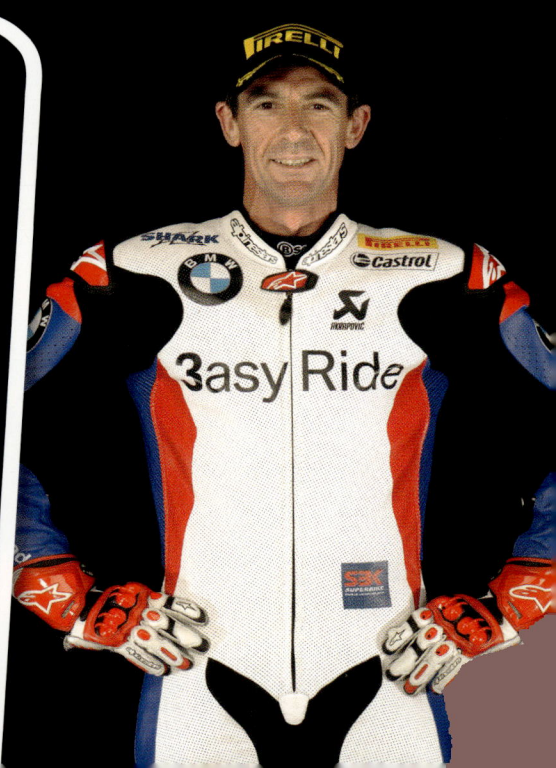

CASTROL HONDA

The largest motorcycle manufacturer in the world is almost obligated to compete in World Superbike, and Honda's participation in the production based series is handled by their European division and the Dutch Ten Kate team. Thanks to sponsorship from Castrol, the team was able to field a two rider lineup for 2011, as they await a completely new version of the CBR 1000 RR for next year, which will again make use of an inline four-cylinder engine.

The team's lead rider was Jonathan Rea, a talented young Briton who unfortunately missed several rounds due to injury. Rea still managed to win two races, one at Assen and one at Imola, while his teammate Ruben Xaus didn't fare as well, the victim of numerous crashes and some injury woes of his own.

Jonathan Rea (above) was born in Ballymena, on February 2nd, 1987, while Ruben Xaus was born of February 18, 1972, in Barcellona. 2011 was the final year of competition for the current version of the CBR 1000 RR, which will be replaced next season by an updated design.

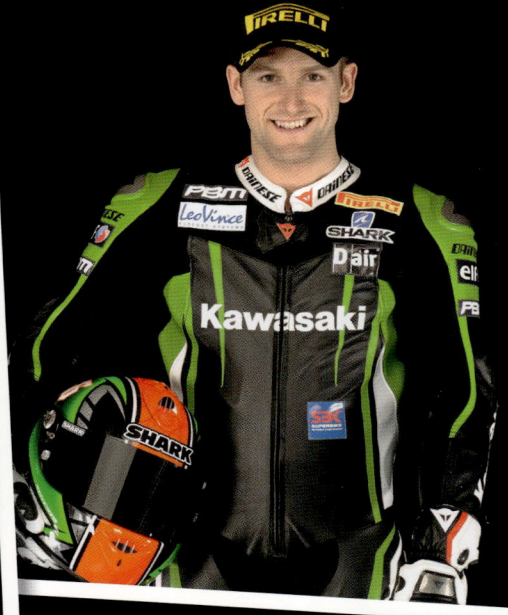

The presentation of the ZX-10R, which took place last season at the Nürburgring, was oriented towards World Superbike competition in 2011. The results might have been slightly below expectations, but some good performances were still recorded by Tom Sykes (at right). Making his Superbike debut was Joan Lascorz (center). Still hampered by his 2010 crash at Phillip Island was Chris Vermeulen.

KAWASAKI Racing Team Superbike

Perhaps the most highly anticipated team of the season, thanks to the considerable amount of winter testing performed with their new bike. Kawasaki was unfortunate, however, in that they couldn't fully rely on the services of Chris Vermeulen, still feeling the effects of a serious injury. The Anglo-Japanese team therefore focused their efforts on Tom Sykes, a British rider his third year of WSBK competition, who managed to secure a Superpole and race win at the Nürburgring. Alongside him was rookie Joan Lascorz, who demonstrated considerable potential in the Supersport category. The new bike proved to be quite formidable in its first year of competition, and the efforts of Kawasaki designers to create a more race and performance oriented ZX-10R, particularly with the Superbike series in mind, seem to have paid off.

PATA Racing Team Aprilia

Born this season out of the fusion between two longstanding WSBK teams, PATA Racing – named after their principle sponsor – chose to shoot for the top, leasing an Aprilia RSV4R, and putting it in the experienced hands of Noriyuki Haga. The Japanese rider was looking to rebound from a disappointing 2010 season with Ducati, and the team was further supported by engineers employed directly by the Italian manufacturer. After some positive winter test results had raised expectations for the team, the Japanese rider initially struggled before making his way forward in the latter stages of the season. The best finishes for Haga were a pair of second places, which probably belie the true potential of both the rider and the team. Nori eventually ended the year eighth in the World Superbike championship points standings.

Noriyuki Haga was born on March 2nd, 1975, in Nagoya. He is one of the most experienced riders in World Superbike. The Japanese rider campaigned the Aprilia RSV4R for Team PATA Racing, after recently racing for Yamaha and Ducati.

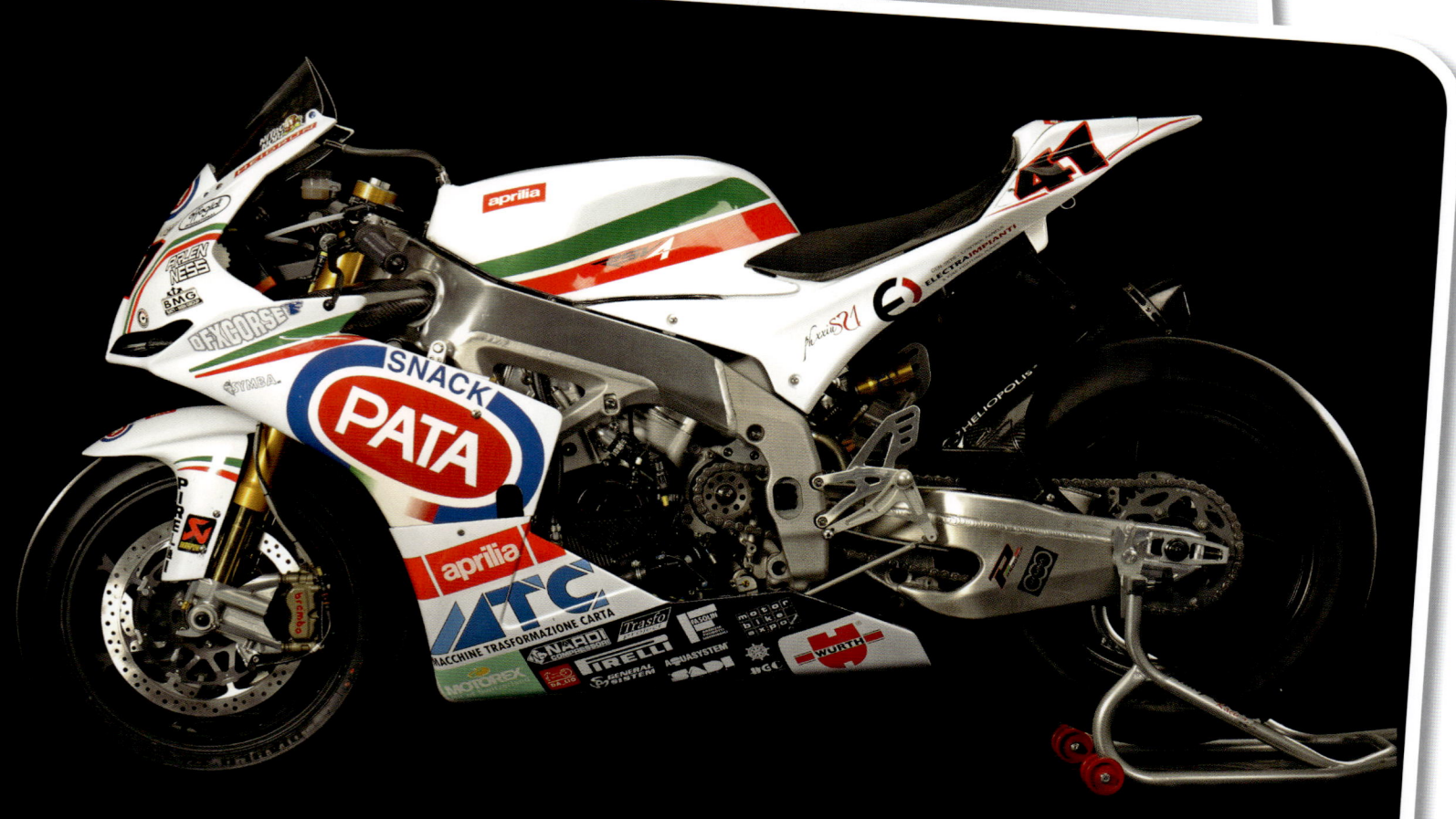

Maxime Berger, 22 years old, was born on June 27th, 1989, in Dijon. He was the European Superstock 600 Champion in 2007 on a Yamaha R6. His best SBK result, in his debut season, was a seventh place at Portimao.

SUPERSONIC Racing Team

Joining World Superbike in 2010, after considerable success at the national level, team Supersonic chose Italian rider Luca Scassa for their debut season.

The young rider's progress was halted slightly by injuries, and for 2011 they turned the bike over to Frenchman Maxime Berger.

Using equipment from Ducati, the Italian team allowed the young rider – making his Superbike and twin-cylinder debut – to gain experience and score a respectable 64 championship points, good for sixteenth place in the standings.

The team's best result (Berger was their only rider) was a seventh place finish in race 1, during the season ending round at Portimao.

TEAM Effenbert-Liberty Racing

A completely new operation (even if many of the team members are veterans of the World Superbike paddock) making their debut for 2011. Sponsored principally by Effenbert beer, produced in the Czech Republic, the team began the season with high ambitions, betting heavily on Jakub Smrz, one of the fastest (and most spectacular) riders over a single flying lap, and Frenchman Sylvain Guintoli, looking to continue his progress after finishing the 2010 season strongly.

The team, which fielded a pair of Ducati 1198's, concluded the season with Guintoli sixth in points (his best results were a pair of second place finishes at the Nürburgring and Portimao) and Smrz in fourteenth place overall (he too managing a pair of second place results, at Donington Park and Salt Lake City).

Sylvain Guintoli (above), 29 years old from Montelimar, came to World Superbike in 2010. Rather inconsistent, but considerably fast, was Jakub Smrz, 28 years old from Ceské Budejovice, who provided some of the most exciting moments of 2011.

TEAM Pedercini

Another historic name in the World Superbike paddock, the team has been running "privateer" Kawasakis for several seasons now (after having previously used Ducatis). The squad, led by Donato and Lucio Pedercini, fielded riders Roberto Rolfo and Mark Aitchison, who had their own unique roles within the team. The former, a Superbike and Grand Prix veteran, was brought onboard for his experience and feedback, as the team was getting to grips with brand new equipment this year. The latter, a young Australian making his WSBK debut, was chosen for his hard charging nature, and he didn't disappoint. The Italian team has very close ties to the Japanese manufacturer's European headquarters, which allowed them to participate in the winter tests alongside the factory squad.

Roberto Rolfo, born in Torino on March 23rd, 1980, was expected to lead the team, but (injuries aside) could do no better than an eleventh place finish at Phillip Island. Mark Aitchison (Gosford, November 22nd, 1983), instead managed a ninth place result at Imola.

TEAM Suzuki Alstare

Suzuki has been a consistent presence in World Superbike, as has been team Alstare, led by Francesco and Patricia Batta. After winning the World Championship in 2005 with Troy Corser, the team continued to rely on equipment form the Japanese manufacturer, this year fielding a single rider operation for Michel Fabrizio, who was coming off a disappointing 2010 season with Ducati (despite a win at Kyalami).

Early in the year Fabrizio scored a podium in race 2 at Monza, and regularly featured in the top five, but he was later slowed by technical issues and crashes, eventually knocking him out of the top ten in championship points.
Further hampering the Belgian team was the diminished support from Suzuki, who showed limited interest in Superbike despite the passion and effort put in by Batta.

Born on Septembe 17th, 1984, in Frascati (Rome), Michel Fabrizio has raced in WSBK for Honda, Ducati and Suzuki. His best season was in 2009, when he finished third in points behind Ben Spies and Noriyuki Haga.

Marco Melandri – born in Ravenna, on August 7th, 1982 – was the lead rider for Yamaha in 2011, and partnered with Eugene Laverty (Toombridge, June 3rd, 1986). The Italian finished the year second in points, while the Irishman was fourth.

YAMAHA World Superbike Team

The 2011 season was certainly a positive one for Yamaha – highlighted by second place finishes in both the Constructors' and Riders' (with Melandri) World Championships – but it was, unfortunately, overshadowed by the announcement that they would be pulling their official team out of the series. A development that was hard to swallow, not only due to the negative implications for the series itself, but also because of the proud and successful tradition the manufacturer from Iwata had obtained in WSBK. Yamaha's 2011 campaign was managed by their European headquarters and spearheaded by Marco Melandri, a young rider who nevertheless has considerable experience, who managed four race wins on the season, putting him second overall in points. Also performing very well was his teammate, young Irishman Eugene Laverty, who was making the step up to Superbike after performing extremely well in Superport: he finished the season fourth overall in points.

BIKES 2011

SEVEN HORSES

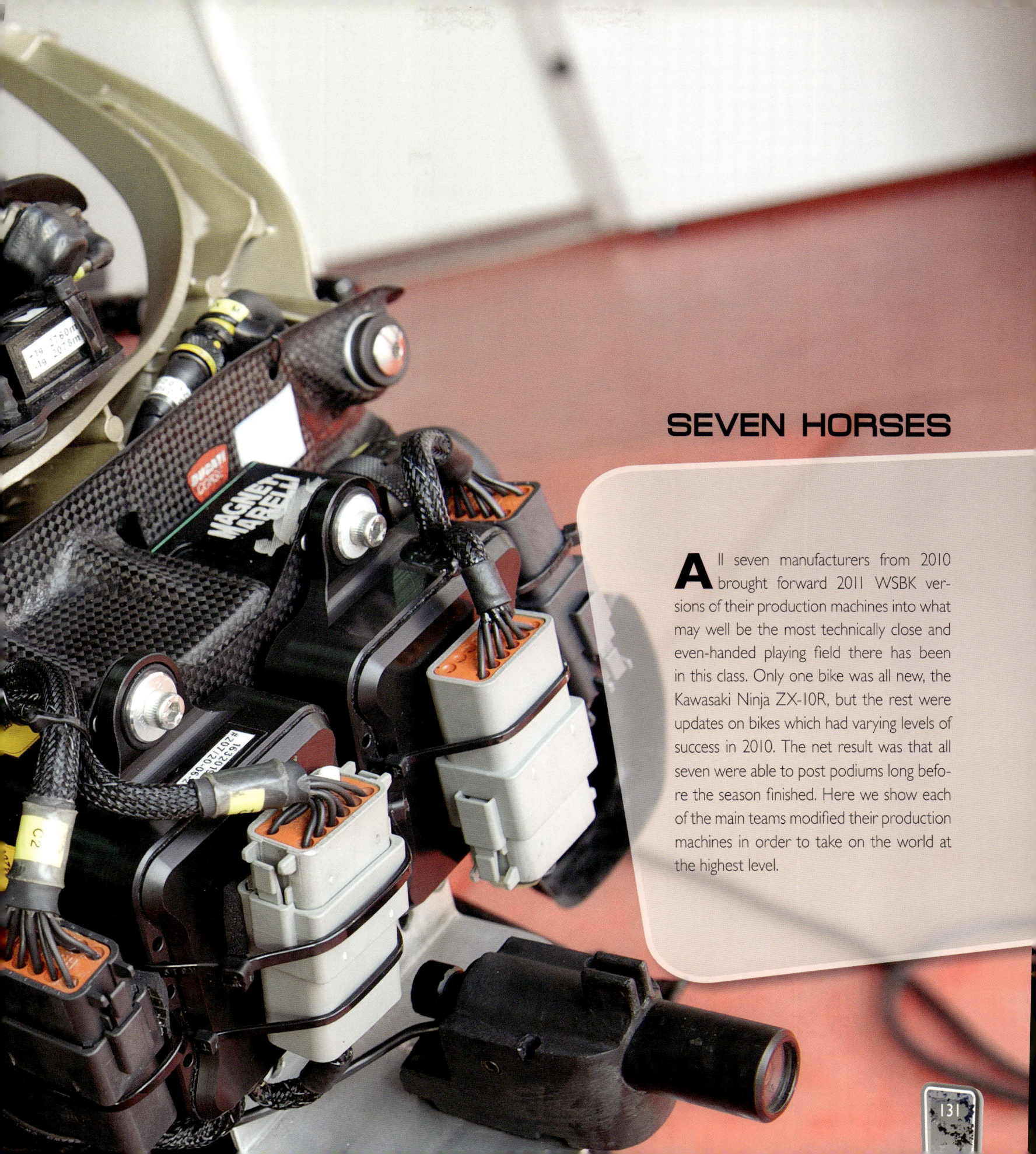

All seven manufacturers from 2010 brought forward 2011 WSBK versions of their production machines into what may well be the most technically close and even-handed playing field there has been in this class. Only one bike was all new, the Kawasaki Ninja ZX-10R, but the rest were updates on bikes which had varying levels of success in 2010. The net result was that all seven were able to post podiums long before the season finished. Here we show each of the main teams modified their production machines in order to take on the world at the highest level.

APRILIA

Aprilia RSV4 Factory SBK

The championship-winning machine that so dominated in 2010 changed very little this year. The main step was initially a rearward one, as the complete gear driven camshaft system, which appeared from Miller onwards in 2010, was excluded from the 2011 regulations.

There was actually no less power than last year, maybe even more, but only because of other detail improvements to the whole package.

There would have been still more horses had the gear driven cams stayed and of course a little more frequent maintenance is needed on the chain system than with the gear system alone. All the same, it has not proved to a weak spot as such in probably the strongest engine out there. Certainly, the title of king of the top speed was not compromised on the Aprilia.

One main step up in engine spec came at Monza, but that had more to do with improving durability than chasing performance. The adoption of stock fuel pumps and injectors also made no real difference to output, as once more a new technical challenge brought in to reduce costs has led to no change in final results.

An extra three kilos compared to 2010, due to rule changes, sees the Aprilia easily meet the 165 kg limit, with a price of around 3,000 Euro per kilo/per bike saved on lightweight parts.

The main focus of development for Aprilia was simple, make the bike work at the kind of bumpy, undulating, simply more old-fashioned circuits it had struggled at in the past. As far as they were concerned, that is mission accomplished in 2011.

Aprilia designed and built the electronics system with a reprogrammed set of parameters to make the bike much more rideable on and off the throttle, with the ignition timing and the throttle butterflies both altered to help with engine braking on corner entry.

Virtually everything inside or outside the engine, including electronics, is an Aprilia Racing part. Noriyuki Haga's Pata Aprilia privateer bike, according to Aprilia boss Luigi Dall'Igna, is the same as the factory one, except Haga prefers the TRVP25 front Öhlins forks, not the more modern TRSP25 units used by Biaggi and Camier. The rear swingarm was the same in 2011 as it was in 2010.

An Aprilia clutch was used on the factory bike, simply because Aprilia has so much experience in this area.

Engine power was around 220+ bhp at 15,000 rpm, with a compression ratio of 14.5:1.

ENGINE	
Type	65° V4 cylinder across the frame, 4-stroke, liquid cooling system, double overhead camshaft (DOHC), four valves per cylinder
Displacement	999 cc
Bore x Stroke	78 x 52.3 mm
Compression Ratio	14.5:1
Fuelling/Ignition	Variable-height intake ducts controlled by engine control unit, electronic injection with 8 injectors and latest-generation ride-by-wire and inertial input technology
Gearbox	Six-speed cassette gearbox
Maximum Power	220+ bhp @ 15,000 rpm
CYCLE PARTS	
Chassis	Adjustable, aluminium dual beam with pressed and cast sheet elements
Suspension	Öhlins 42mm TRSP25 forks, RSP 40
Brakes	Brembo Evo callipers, back to Lithium Aluminium for Biaggi after Donington. 320 mm Brembo 'H'-Type discs
Wheelbase	23 litres (variable)
Dimensions	2,050 mm
Fuel tank	23 litri (variabile)
Kerb Mass	165 kg

Aprilia engine lost none of its potency despite losing its gear-driven camshaft system. Densely packaged, narrow in width and length across the cylinders, the 65° four was designed as half road bike-half race bike from the outset.

BIKES 2011

*Rear swingarm was made in-house, the electronics and much of the clutch also, or to designs from Aprilia Racing.
Without bodywork you can see how the chassis spars embrace the engine closely, without having to be angled outwards.*

The 'H-type' (or 'T-type') Brembo disc brake bobbins were originally developed with Aprilia for the 250GP class, so Aprilia uses those ones rather than the more traditional floating circular bobbins joining the rotors and discs together.
The fuel tank shape has been changed for rider comfort, starting from the very end of last year.

135

22,9 Ltr

> Fuel tank shape and size was played with to try and get the weight balance of the bike moved back a little. The very narrow nature of the BMW engine and chassis layout was a key to its original design, which makes it very aerodynamic.

BMW

BMW S 1000 RR

The one thing that dominates the design of the S1000RR is its engine. A strange thing to say maybe when it is simply a conventional – if narrow – inline four? It is the radical 80 x 49.7 mm bore and stroke figures and low reciprocating mass, plus quick moving and lightweight 'finger' cam operation, that means this unit is small in size and revs to the max. Now peaking at over 14,000 rpm the engine is good for over 220 bhp. A 14.5:1 compression ratio is up from last year.

The 2011 bike went back to a long exhaust design, exiting on the right, to make engine rideability better, smoothing out power.

An STM slipper clutch is fitted and much work is being done on reducing drive train backlash to help under engine braking and on-off-on-off throttle applications.

BMW is very proud of its own electronics hardware, even if the main connectors are quite big by modern standards. Software is still the soft point, simply because others have much more experience than BMW, claims the engineering staff. A 2D dash is used on the home-brewed BMW system. The GPS sensor on the BMW had to have its cover removed after the Infront onboard TV cameras were mounted to each and every bike. With the cover on, the GPS signal was too weak to work properly.

In general terms the main task for the engineers this year was to get more weight heading backwards not forward, and around 2-3% more weight is on the rear this year. This has been done partly by relocating certain things, like the battery and EFI computer. They are also finding it hard to match their entire transmission and electronic set-up to Haslam's hard braking, hard throttle-closing, riding style. Too much weight on the front overall has left the BMW dancing with its rear wheel in the air, and has caused Haslam to reputedly switch it down to almost nothing to improve corner entry.

Changes in geometry and ride height have helped, but the problem is still there to some degree. Even the fuel tank shape was changed to help this aspect of performance.

Amazingly at this level, and in a team that has had the most exotic swingarms in the past, the 2011 version is the completely stock one, simply lifted from the road-bike. It is heavier than the racing versions but it does help absorb bumps better and the weight is not that important now each bike has an extra 3 kg to carry compared to 2010.

ENGINE	
Type	Transverse four cylinder four-stroke, liquid-cooled
Displacement	999 cc
Bore x Stroke	80 x 49.7 mm
Compression Ratio	14.5:1
Fuelling/Ignition	Dell'Orto injection 48 mm/BMW RSM5 EFI, ride-by-wire
Gearbox	six speed
Maximum Power	220 bhp @ over 14,000 rpm
Clutch	STM slipper type

CYCLE PARTS	
Chassis	Alum. twin-spar 'bridge' type
Suspension	42 mm TRSP25 forks, RSP 40
Brakes	Brembo callipers, Evo and Aluminium Lithium types, 320 mm rotors, 4-piston callipers. Nissin used by Corser until Assen race, also 320 mm rotors
Wheelbase	1440 mm (variable)
Dimensions	2056 mm
Fuel tank	23 litres
Kerb Mass	165 kg

BIKES 2011

Stripped down (above) you can see the split fuel tank and stock swingarm. Engine looks tall but has most extreme bore in the class.
OZ Wheels and Marchesini units were both evaluated. Brembo brakes came after Haslam requested them.

Suspension is now the most modern type from Öhlins, front and rear. Wheels are now Marchesini, despite the official partnership with OZ Wheels, as they simply work better right now exiting corners. Brakes are whatever Brembos Haslam (and now Corser) want – the Evo type or the Aluminium Lithium version. Corser started on Nissin but changed to Brembo, and uses the standard ones as he likes them better than the newer Evo callipers right now.

139

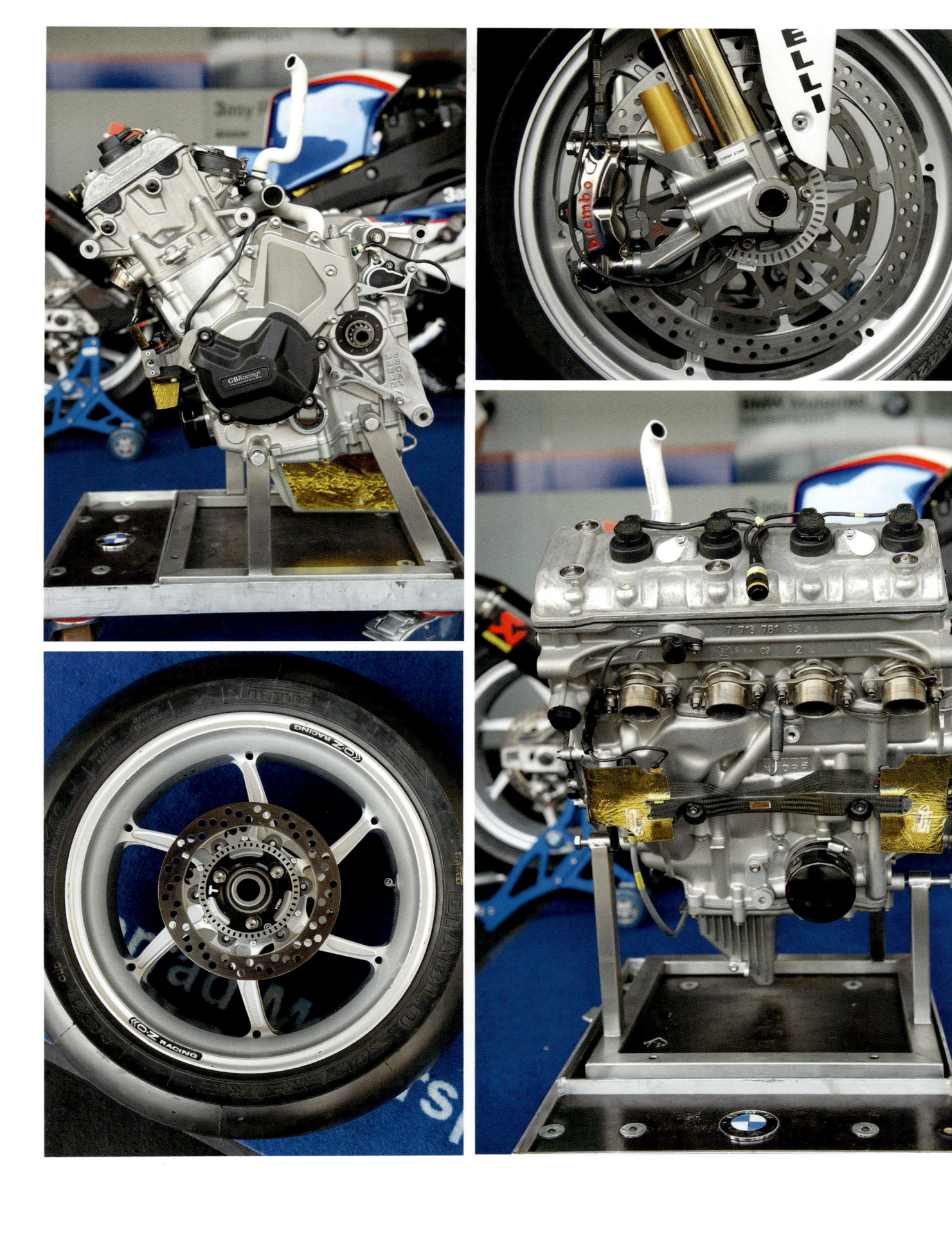

DUCATI

Ducati 1198 RS11

The unique situation of having no factory team this year means that Carlos Checa started his season with a better bike than he had in 2010, but not better than the bike used by the Xerox factory team back then. It's called the RS11 now, as there is no factory machine to continue the F-prefix naming code.

The 106 x 67.9 mm engine was obviously lower revving than the fours, and had a few less horses at the top, but it was a well-known quantity. With Carlos flying the bike, and the team getting It set right every weekend, Checa could use 100% of his performance pretty much 100% of the time.

The booming twin's torque is an asset of course but Ducati Corse Director Ernesto Marinelli bristles when you mention that, with both he and Checa claiming that the reason for the class-leading success is more to do with the chassis set-up at the front – meaning Checa can enter the corners faster, on a tighter line, and still not pressurise the tyre too much. Result is? He can pass under braking when others cannot, and his consistent bike performance lets him ride free from mistakes.

Technical aspects which are the same as 2010 are the Magneti Marelli Marvel4 EFI, and IWP 162 + IWP 189 twin injectors per cylinder fuelling control system. No fancy new MHT version needed, according to Marinelli.

50 mm air-intake restrictors (mounted below the butterfly) were part of the rules, remained a constant and therefore the 200 CV from the engine (at the crank) came in at 11,000 rpm. Power was transmitted by a Ducati dry clutch system.

New exhausts and cams came on stream to match in with new electronics and maps at the start of the season for Althea's new 'factory privateers'. Ducati is in the habit of not making updates in any season unless it is for safety or durability reasons.

For the chassis, a Ducati fabricated single sided swingarm held things up at the back, while at the front the same forks as the factory boys used last year dealt with the bumps. Also, the rear shock was unchanged, but it is still the best of Öhlins material.

The brake discs on the Ducati were widely spaced from the centre line to allow them to stay cool in use, the opposite of other manufacturers' ideas about tucking them in to improve aerodynamics.

The new regulation weight of 165 kg was easily achievable because that's what Ducatis used to weigh by regulation anyway, and the lack of titanium etc. cut costs in 2011.

The balancing rules state that the Ducati can be more than 165 kg by regulation if they get too many points compared to the

ENGINE	
Type	4-stroke L-twin 90°
Displacement	1198 cc
Bore x Stroke	106 x 67.9 mm
Compression Ratio	Not quoted
Fuelling/Ignition	Electronic Ignition-injection ECU Magneti Marelli Marvel4, Magneti Marelli electronic injection system, elliptical throttle bodies with air-restrictor below the butterfly 50 mm equivalent diameter. Magneti Marelli IWP162+IWP189, twin injectors each cylinder Exhaust: Termignoni stainless steel/titanium
Gearbox	Six speed/dry multiplate slipper clutch with hydraulic control
Maximum Power	200 CV @11,000 rpm
Maximum Torque	Not quoted
Top Speed	310 kmph with restrictor

CYCLE PARTS	
Chassis	Tubular steel trellis frame
Suspension	42 mm TRVP25 upside-down Öhlins forks, single-side alum. swingarm, with Öhlins RSP 40
Brakes	Brembo radial P4X34-38 calliper, two 320 mm floating discs on round floating bobbins, Brembo P2X34 calliper, one 218 mm disc
Wheelbase	1435 mm
Dimensions	2055 mm
Fuel tank	23.9 litres
Kerb Mass	165 kg

Big Ducati intakes with regulation air restrictors inside the rubbers. A real feat of modernization over generations, this engine made up for in torque and layout what it lost in top end revs and power.

BIKES 2011

Dry clutch as always and note 'high-tech' bent washer holding on the retaining nut… Trick nose fairing sub frame holds instrument board. Belt drive has tensioners to keep the timing right for the desmo system.

fours, and the restrictors can go down to 46 mm or up to 52 mm, or even be removed altogether, again if the balancing rules dictate they should.

The main tune-up on the bike this year has come directly from the throttle hand and brain of Carlos Checa, according to Ducati Corse.

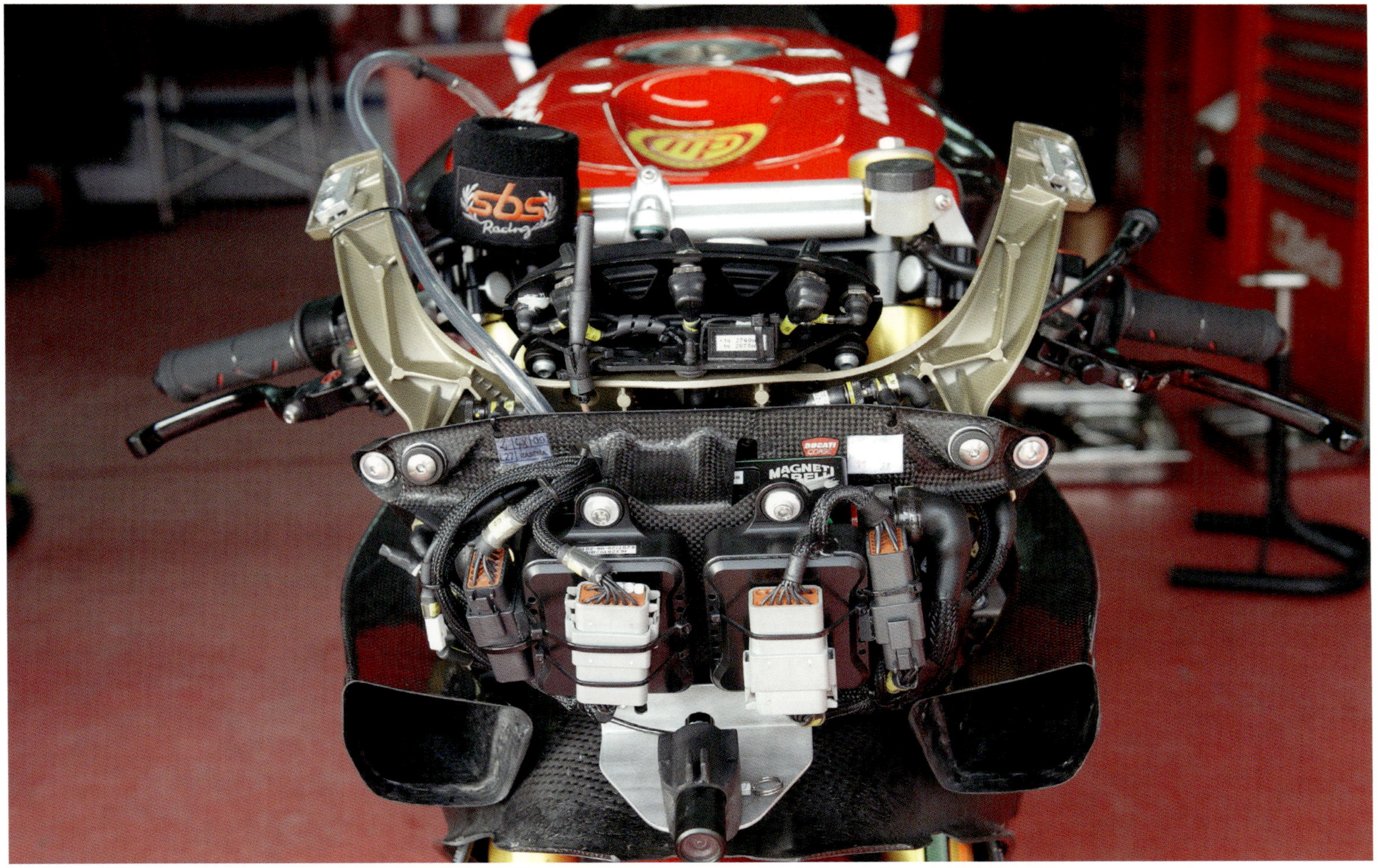
sbs
Racing
MAGNETI

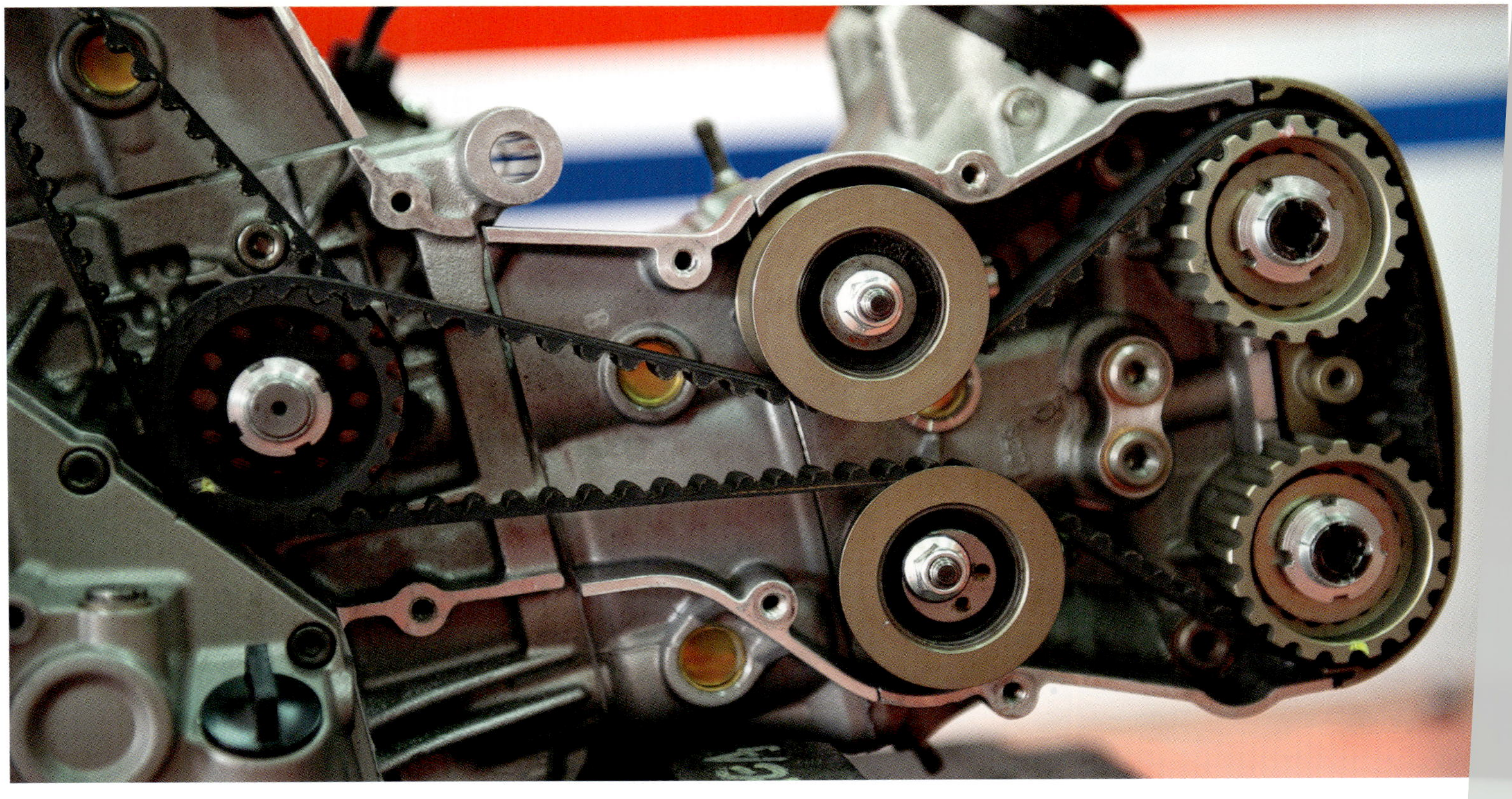

144

Still capable of championship wins despite an ancient overall design (left). Details, details… Plumber's nightmare (top), top line (if not radical) Brembo brake set-up (middle), a vipers' nest of electronics from Marelli (bottom).

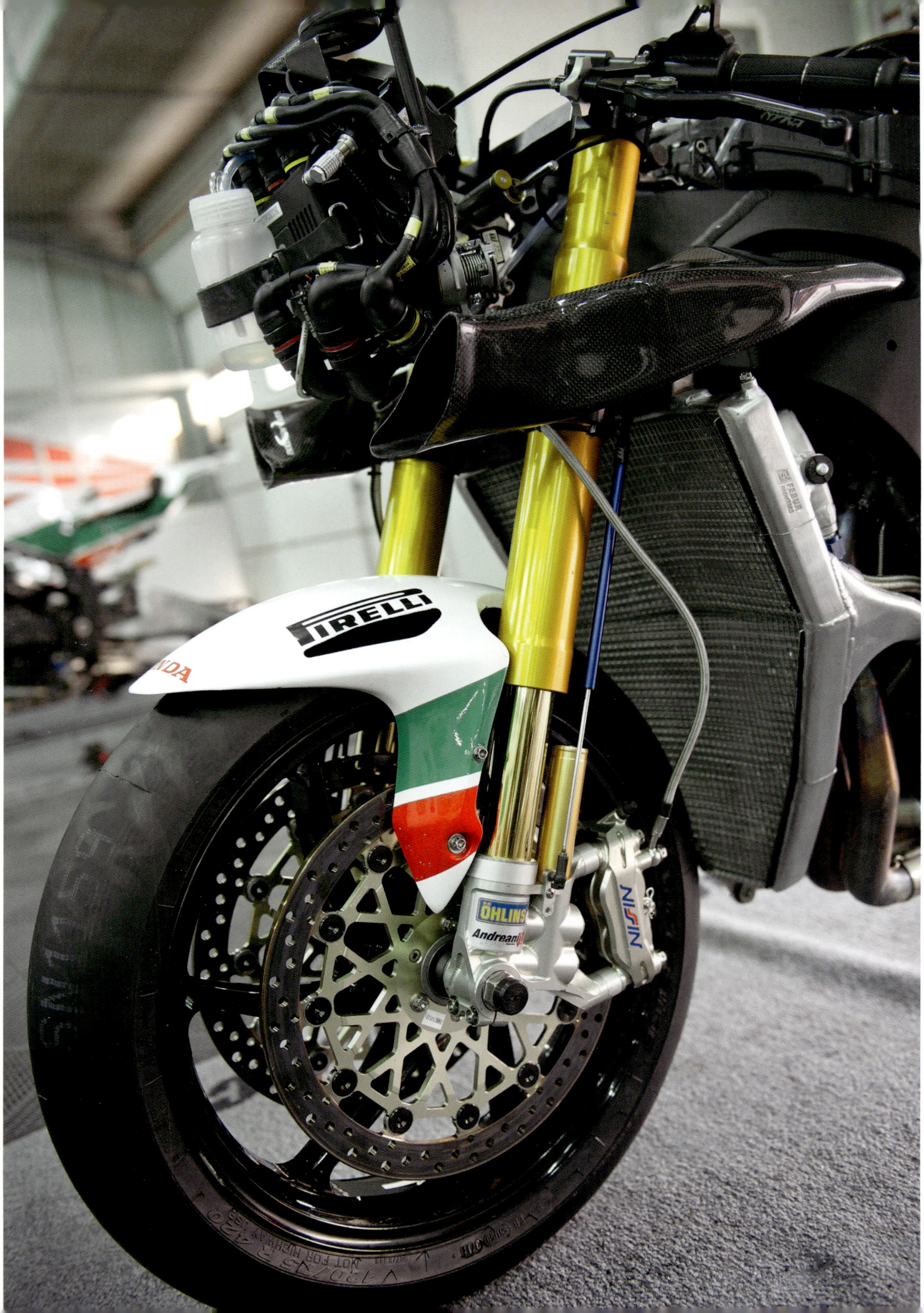
PIRELLI
ÖHLINS
NISSIN

Honda

Honda CBR1000RR

Ever the mavericks: Ten Kate opted for equipment the others seldom used on their Castrol Honda, most notably Nissin brake calipers and Yutaka brake discs. Forks were often a generation behind their rivals, but the latest units were used in testing.

ENGINE	
Type	Liquid cooled transverse 4-stroke 16-valves DOHC four-cylinder
Displacement	999.8 cc
Bore x Stroke	76 x 55.1 mm
Compression Ratio	Not quoted
Fuelling/Ignition	46 mm Pi research Pectel
Gearbox	Six speed
Maximum Power	220+ bhp
Aircleaner	Sprintfilter
CYCLE PARTS	
Chassis	Diamond aluminium composite twin-spar
Suspension	43 mm fork called RSP25 (Rod solid piston) and RSP36 (Rod solid piston, 36 mm displacement) rear shock.
Brakes	Yutaka 320 mm discs/four pad Nissin callipers
Wheelbase	adjustable
Wheels	PVM Magnesium
Dimensions	2080 mm long
Fuel tank	22 litres
Kerb Mass	165 kg

Now a bit long in the tooth, the CBR1000RR still won races in 2011, although the main piece missing at the start of the year appeared to be full factory Öhlins support. An obvious omission said some, but it was too costly an item for a team with a limited budget. They upgraded from 2010 of course, but carried on with one generation older kit than their main rivals, looked after by Andreani suspension gurus from Italy, and their own in house team.

Suspension was a major area of change anyway, although not to the level of an Aprilia or Yamaha full factory set-up. The team tested the near full works TRSP43 factory forks at Miller, but with other problems to solve, they dropped them for the more conventional RSP25 (TTX25) material.

A 220 bhp engine had a fair amount of HRC kit parts inside, as well as the work done on them by Ten Kate themselves. There was an HRC kit conrods and pistons, clutch, plus an HRC gearbox.

Sunstar sprockets and a 520 Regina chain were adopted to drive the bike. In the era of stock fuel pumps, the Honda's squeezed its fuel to 3.6 bar before being told when to fire it into the engine. An airbox and two injectors per cylinders and were the stock items, by regulation. PI Research Pectel was again adopted for the engine management, with Ten Kate sending requests to software suppliers Cosworth to update their software strategies. Basically, Ten Kate are the software end users, and Cosworth the suppliers.

The relationship is growing and getting even closer, to the point where they used a ride-by-wire system to win at Imola, first time out.

Both Rea and Xaus used a KR rear swingarm but chatter was still a problem to be overcome by the team most weekends. Ten Kate also tested an HRC 8 hour swingarm at Miller. There were positive and negative areas, but in the end it did not work well with the Pirelli tyres.

The close technical and commercial partnership with Nissin continued in 2011, with a new four-piston caliper tested in the winter and approved for use all year.

They remained gripping 320 mm rotors, not the 330 mm units they once use. Brake discs themselves were from Yutaka, a new type for 2011.

147

BIKES 2011

More road engine than race engine, but still potent. PVM wheels another Ten Kate favourite. Engine cases/crash protectors. Note vertical quick-shifter.
Opposite page: Short Arrow exhaust and gorgeous swingarms were used by both riders all year. Stripped down CBR – the UJM, 2011-style.

149

KAWASAKI

Kawasaki Ninja ZX-10R

The whole Ninja ZX-10R world Superbike machine was a novelty in 2011 and of course as well as a more modern engine and (slightly more modern) engine position, the biggest change was to the rear suspension design.

Called a Horizontal Back Link system it saw the rear shock laid down almost horizontally front-to-back, entirely free from being buried inside the chassis somewhere. This kept the unit cooler, more accessible and adjustable, plus with a top connector bolted straight onto the transverse rear chassis spar, and finally a triangular link between shock bottom and swingarm, to give rising rate. The bike was unmistakeably different from the rest in this regard. It improved mass centralisation, gave smoother operation, and being mounted off centre it allowed the exhaust more room for a less fussy run towards the outside world.

Quite a number of swingarms were tried early in the year, but that constant evaluation settled down after Assen and now all three riders use the same version, while still working on linkages and suspension settings track-to-track.

The suspension itself was unique to Kawaski's factory squad this year. A full time Showa tech was on hand at races and oversaw the performance of the BPF-4 front forks, new on the insides and with a whopping 47 mm diameter, providing 120 mm travel. There is a new internal development with pressure and less friction than 2010.

The main ease of use for the latest Showa rear shock systems is that all the main adjustments that do not need removal to take place but can be adjusted via small screwdriver slots for compression and rebound. Very simple, very neat.

Last year's triple clamps were used again, new bike or no new bike. Also the new shape (to suit the new horizontal application) T518-BFR system rear shock was a modified version for 2011.

There was some new development on the front forks every six to eight weeks, either in internal spec or stiffness of fork construction. Such are the luxuries of having your own suspension manufacturer to yourself. Both PBM and KHI sides of the operation stated that this full attention to Kawasaki alone was a great help in developing the new bike.

The chassis itself had some gusseting added but tests have been inconclusive so far. Head angle and other geometry settings are still being worked on, but they are not normally changed, other than by clicks and spring settings during a race weekend.

Sophisticated MHT Magneti Marelli system made it onto the new Ninja, as the only new bike of 2011 hit the tracks. Note central intake in its modern design, and mini-bracket under ECU to hold on very angular new nosecone.

ENGINE	
Type	DOHC transverse four-cylinder, four-stroke, liquid cooled
Displacement	999.8 cc
Bore x Stroke	76 x 55 mm
Compression Ratio	Not quoted
Fuelling/Ignition	Keihin 47 mm throttle bodies, Magneti Marelli MHT with Marelli dash and custom software
Gearbox	Six speed
Maximum Power	215 bhp @ 15,500 rpm
CYCLE PARTS	
Chassis	Alum. twin spar, horiz. back link, progressive
Suspension	Showa BPF-4, 47 mm diameter, stroke 120 mm with triple adjusters-rebound, compression, and preload. Rear shock Showa T518-BFR system, with triple adjuster
Brakes	Brembo 305 mm discs Aluminium Lithium, T-type, SBS brake pads
Fuel tank	23 litres
Kerb Mass	165 kg

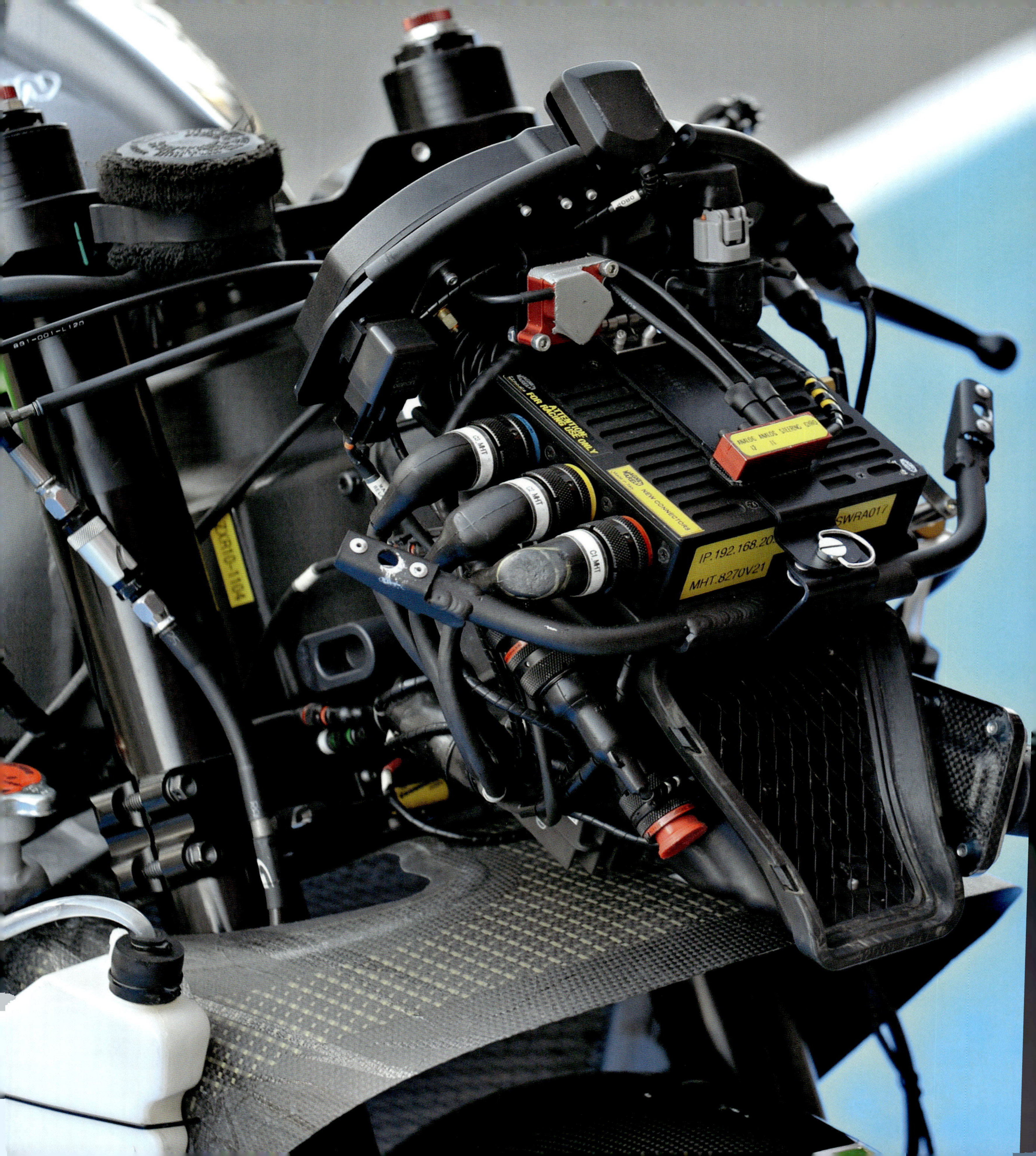
IP.192.168.20
MHT.8270V21
SWRA017
NEW CONNECTORS

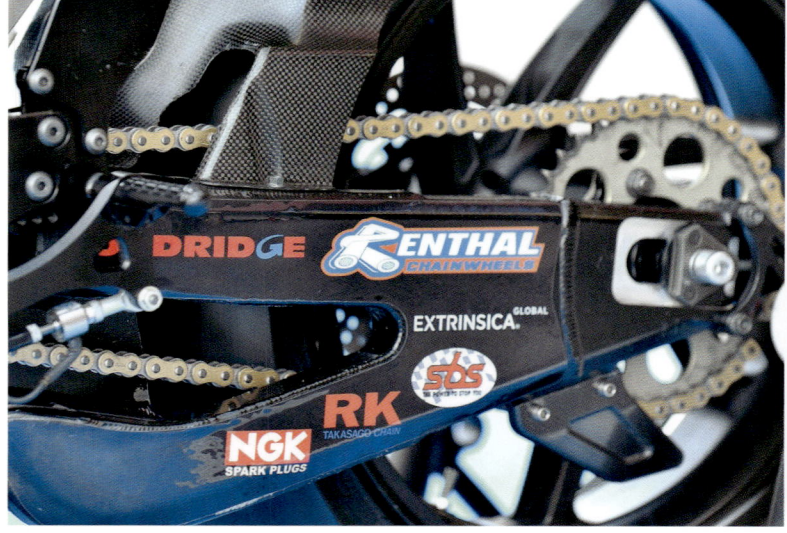

Kawasaki Heavy Engineering indeed on the chassis spars. Rear swingarm went through several re-designs as all new rear suspension system was brought in.
Showa suspension was unique to Kawasaki in 2011, Brembo brakes used throughout.

BIKES 2011

Overall the bike is smaller than the old one, has more weight on the front of the bike but the biggest improvement is turning and holding a line, according to the rider feedback.
A generally better balanced chassis means that the team can now improve the bike overall rather than making one end (front or rear) better at expense of the capability of the other end.
The engine is not as radically positioned as other machines but it has a high clutch position to improve mass centralisation.

Overall, lower, smaller and more modern than the 2010 machine. The high-clutch engine was better for centralizing mass and strengthening engine cases. You can see the end of the rear shock above the footrest hanger, as Kawasaki made one major departure from their peers in that area.

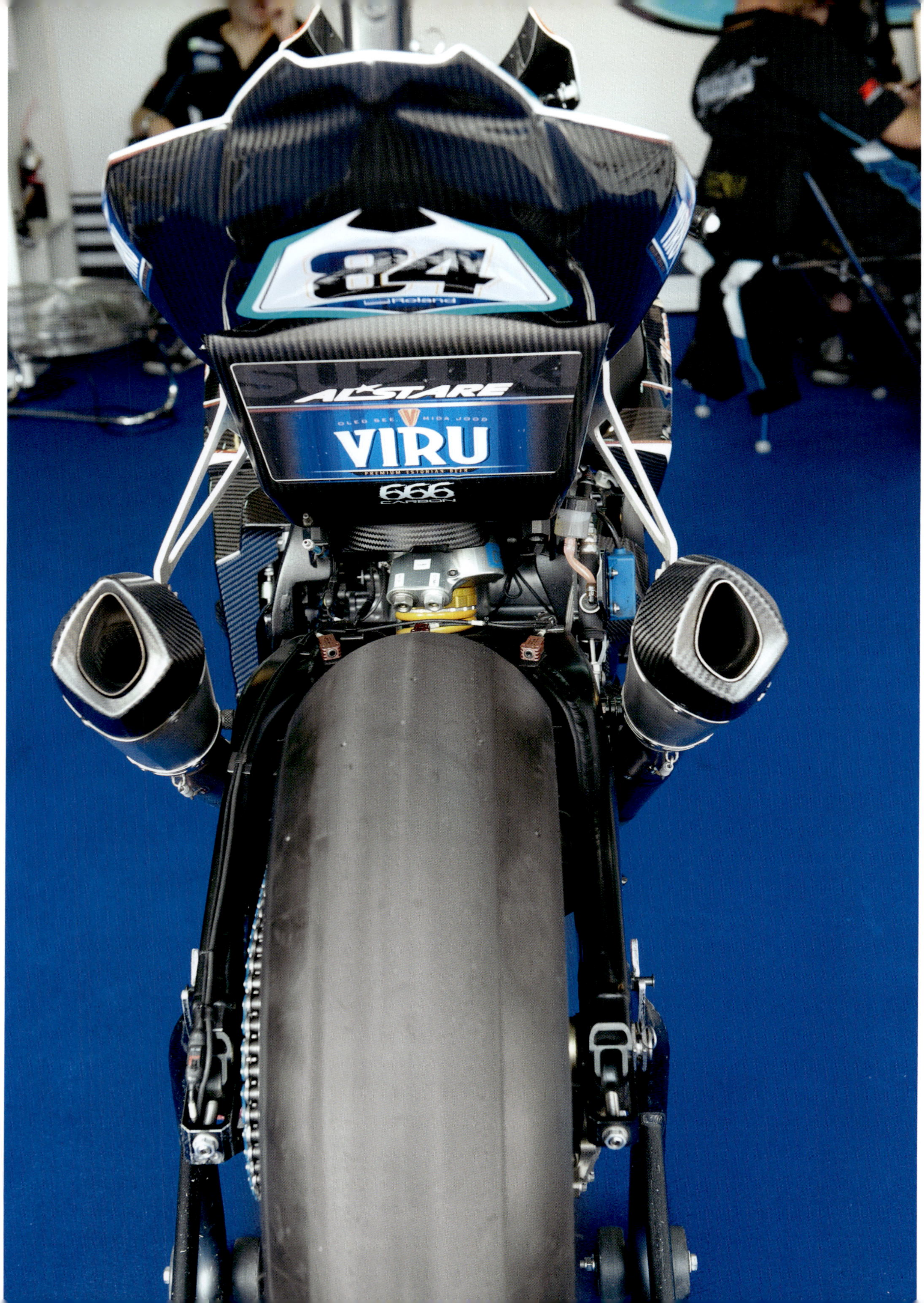
84
SUZUKI
ALSTARE
VIRU
666
CARBON

Suzuki Alstare GSX-R1000K11

Twin Arrow exhausts dominate the rear view of the still-fast Suzuki. With the Kawasaki getting all radical with its rear suspension, the Suzuki was easily the most conventional bike on the grid in 2011.

ENGINE	
Type	Liquid-cooled transverse four-cylinder 4-stroke
Displacement	998.6 cc
Bore x Stroke	74.5 x 57.3 mm
Compression Ratio	14.8:1
Conrods	Pankl/Suzuki
Piston	Pankl/Suzuki
Fuelling/Ignition	Magneti Marelli Marvel4/2D data acquisition
Gearbox	six speed
Maximum Power	207 bhp @13,600 rpm
Maximum Torque	118 Nm
CYCLE PARTS	
Chassis	Twin Spar aluminium chassis
Suspension	Öhlins 42mm RSP25 (Rod solid piston)/RSP 40 (Rod solid piston, 40 mm displacement). Rear shock
Brakes	Brembo Lithium Alum., 320 mm discs with round mounting.
Wheelbase	1420 mm (variable)
Dimensions	not quoted
Fuel tank	24 litres
Kerb Mass	165 kg

For Suzuki, one of the older designs of conventional fours was still a weapon with a sharp edge. It was as much a Belgian bayonet as a samurai sword in 2011, however, as the Alstare team had to use up all their Suzuki material given to them at the end of 2010, and then start out with some of their own stuff, and some material made to their spec by suppliers. The chassis on the 2011 Suzuki may look familiar because it is, almost in its entirety, the same one used by the same team in 2010. Hence it had one generation older forks but the latest rear shock. It all works well, and the Suzuki crew are convinced they have one of the best bikes out there, even now.

The engine has been worked on in 2011, all in-house apparently in the Alstare Engineering workshops. The engine development guys have found more revs, with intake camshaft and duration changes the main developments inside the engine. There is also a new kind of air funnel system inside the airbox, to suit the new cams.

With modded cams you need a new exhaust to make it work at its best, and the design of that Arrow pipe was changed, at the collector box, to give a wider band of power. The end result is more power and torque and the curve is flatter. In the real world, the acceleration performance is also better.

Fuel delivery is now via the regulation standard fuel pump, so no more 5 bar fuel pressure, it's back down to 3 bar – the standard bike's setting.

Some engines raced with Suzuki conrods some with Pankl conrods, but whether the engines are from Suzuki or Alstare the performance is about the same. Only 207 bhp, is the modest claim.

The software in the electronics was also changed to suit the new cam and exhaust mods. The software has been changed three times, the modifications coming for overall different tuning strategies.

The stock Suzuki EFI system features two butterflies. One of them is a ride-by-wire butterfly and one can be opened independently of the other via the engine management to aid engine braking. On the overrun this butterfly control works on all four cylinders.

For the engine management a Magneti Marelli system is used but the data acquisition system is from 2D, because they use 2D in the GP programme and it is what Suzuki wants any feedback to be presented by.

An STM slipper clutch is controlled on

BIKES 2011

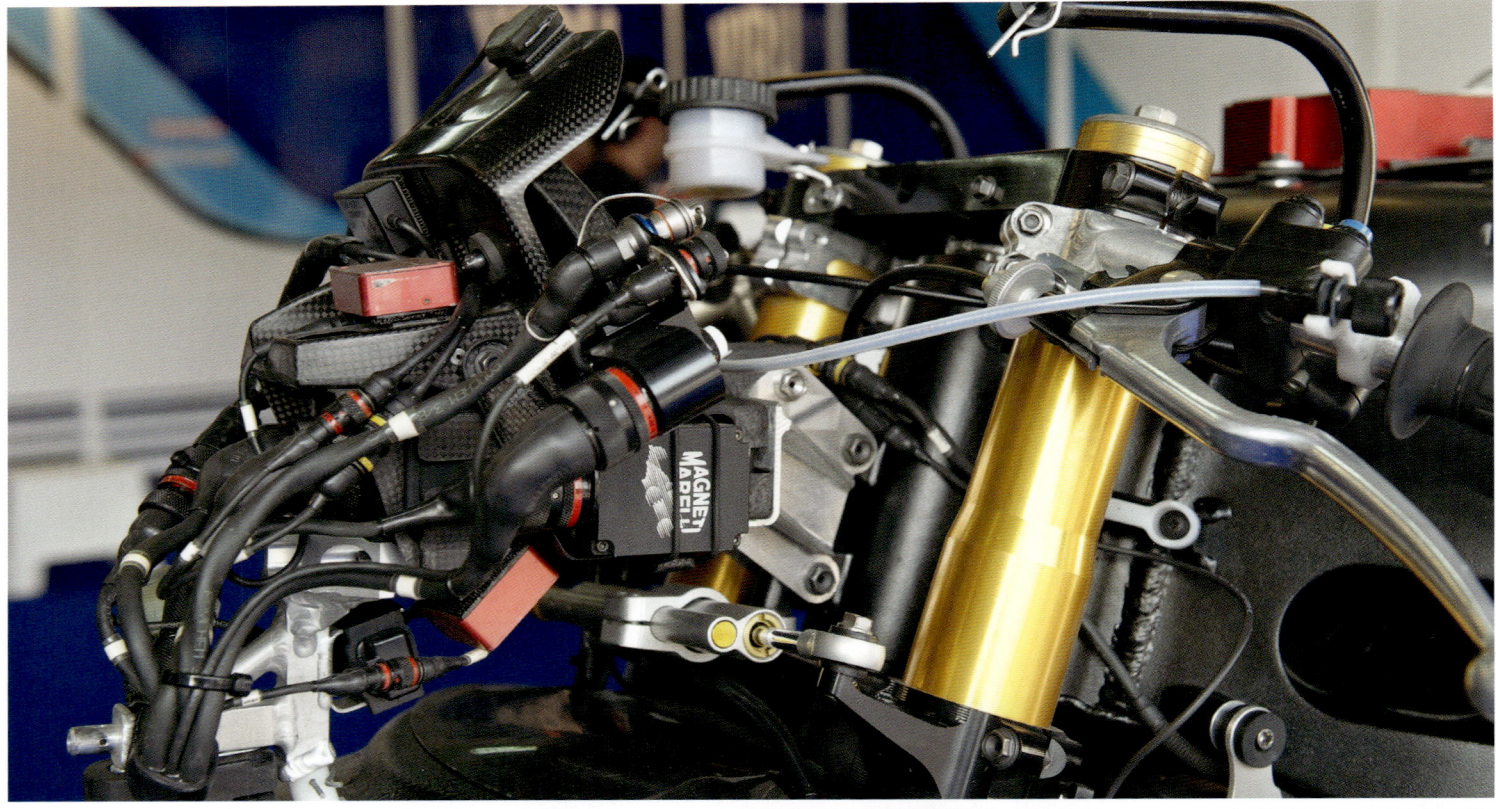

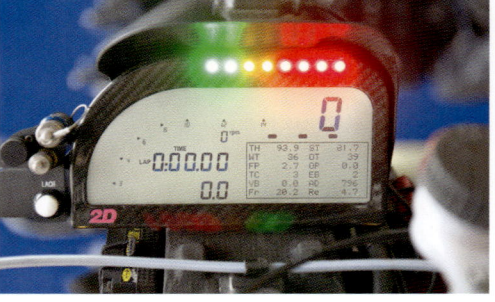

Magneti Marelli electronics but note the 2D display. Suzuki in Japan uses 2D for data so Alstare used a hybrid system again. Brembo brakes and Öhlins suspension, the usual mix. Some new suspension units were tried but others were rejected as not really needed.

the corner entry.

Suzuki does not use the most advanced Öhlins front fork material, preferring the through rod type forks, even though they have evaluated the new stuff in testing.

Suzuki had no problem with mounting or interference from the TV cameras, and Suzuki only use their GPS for data acquisition, not for engine management.

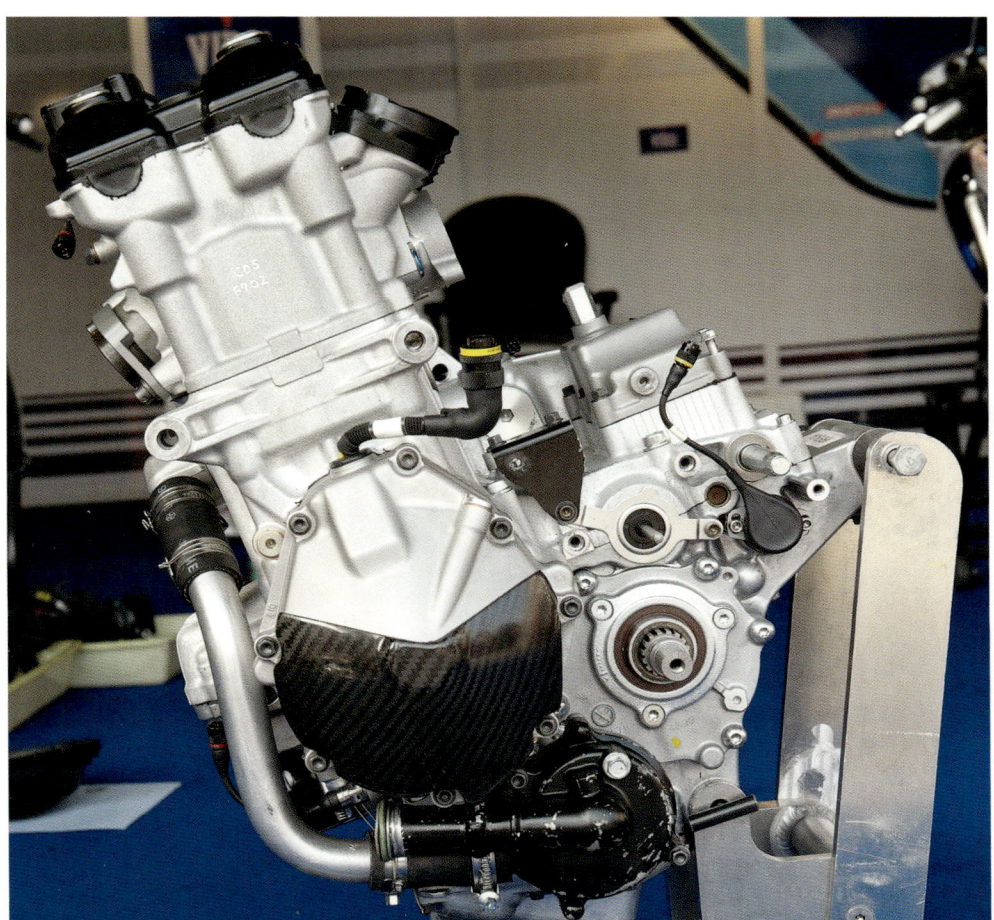

Two sides of the engine show it as a semi-modern affair, with slightly raised clutch but high gearbox. In the chassis the engine is tilted forwards and the split fuel tank also contributed to centralizing mass, and preventing fuel surge.

Yamaha World Superbike YZF-R1

The main change in the powerful and proven R1 racebike in the winter period was a major one. The fuel tank was moved to the standard position to make it lighter on the rear and because the riders asked for a very narrow bike, the rear seat design was smoothed out and the fuel tank shape was changed to suit. The height of the bike is the same as in 2010, but it is narrower.

A deep fuel tank is now split vertically compared to last year, when the fuel tank was under the seat unit, causing problems when the fuel load changed. Now the fuel load is carried in the centre of the bike, where it makes less difference as the fuel level goes down.

The weight is still not quite at the allowed 165 kg, but a smaller batter was adopted and the starter motor was removed, to make the bike close to the limit – 165.3 kg. Yamaha embraced the latest Öhlins front forks, the 42 mm TRSP25. They supposedly helped quite a bit for the braking, and gave more support mid-corner. Old gas forks sometimes pushed back mid-corner.

A new top triple clamp also helps out with mid-corner feel, and is made in magnesium, with slotted sections. It affords greater flexibility in corners but the same stability under braking. The rider feels a better feeling with the bumps, and helps with front tyre contact. This first appeared at the second Phillip Island test, not the first one.

Rear suspension was the same as last year, and the swingarm started the same as 2010. Before Monza for Laverty and in Aragon for Melandri, they went a little bit softer on the swingarm, as the rigidity was changed.

The new YZF-R1 has no rear sub-frame but incorporates a strengthened rear frame.

The bike features the latest Magneti Marelli (MHT) electronic systems with over 30 sensors on the bike to monitor variables such as temperature and pressure of air, oil, water and fuel. The temperature of the brake disc and the tyre is also measured, as well as brake pressure, suspension travel, speed, acceleration, throttle position, camshaft position and crankshaft position – but not the fuel conservancy inputs used in MotoGP. The swing arm is also developed purely for the WSB race bike.

There's also inertial platform, with integrated accelerometer and gyroscope to calculate the bike angle and position, which helps traction control and engine braking strategies.

A test in the winter with standard fuel pump and standard injectors lost no performance and a completely new fuel map was made. The changed intake port on the cylinder head was said to be a good step, matched

Of all the Japanese machines the Yamaha was the one with most outright race ideas thrown at it. May of them stuck, as the redesigned (in WSBK spec at least) R1 became a genuine challenger to the Ducati and Aprilia.

ENGINE	
Type	DOHC transverse four-cylinder four-stroke, cross-plane crank
Displacement	998 cc
Bore x Stroke	78 x 52.2 mm
Compression Ratio	Not quoted
Fuelling/Ignition	Magneti Marelli MHT
Gearbox	Six speed
Maximum Power	230 bhp @ approx 15,000 rpm
CYCLE PARTS	
Chassis	Aluminium Deltabox twin spar aluminium
Suspension	Öhlins 42 mm TRSP25 (Through-rod, solid piston) RSP 40 (Rod solid piston, 40 mm displacement).
Brakes	Brembo 320 mm rotors or 314 mm rotors. H-type bobbins
Wheelbase	1415 mm
Fuel tank:	24 litres
Kerb Mass	165 kg

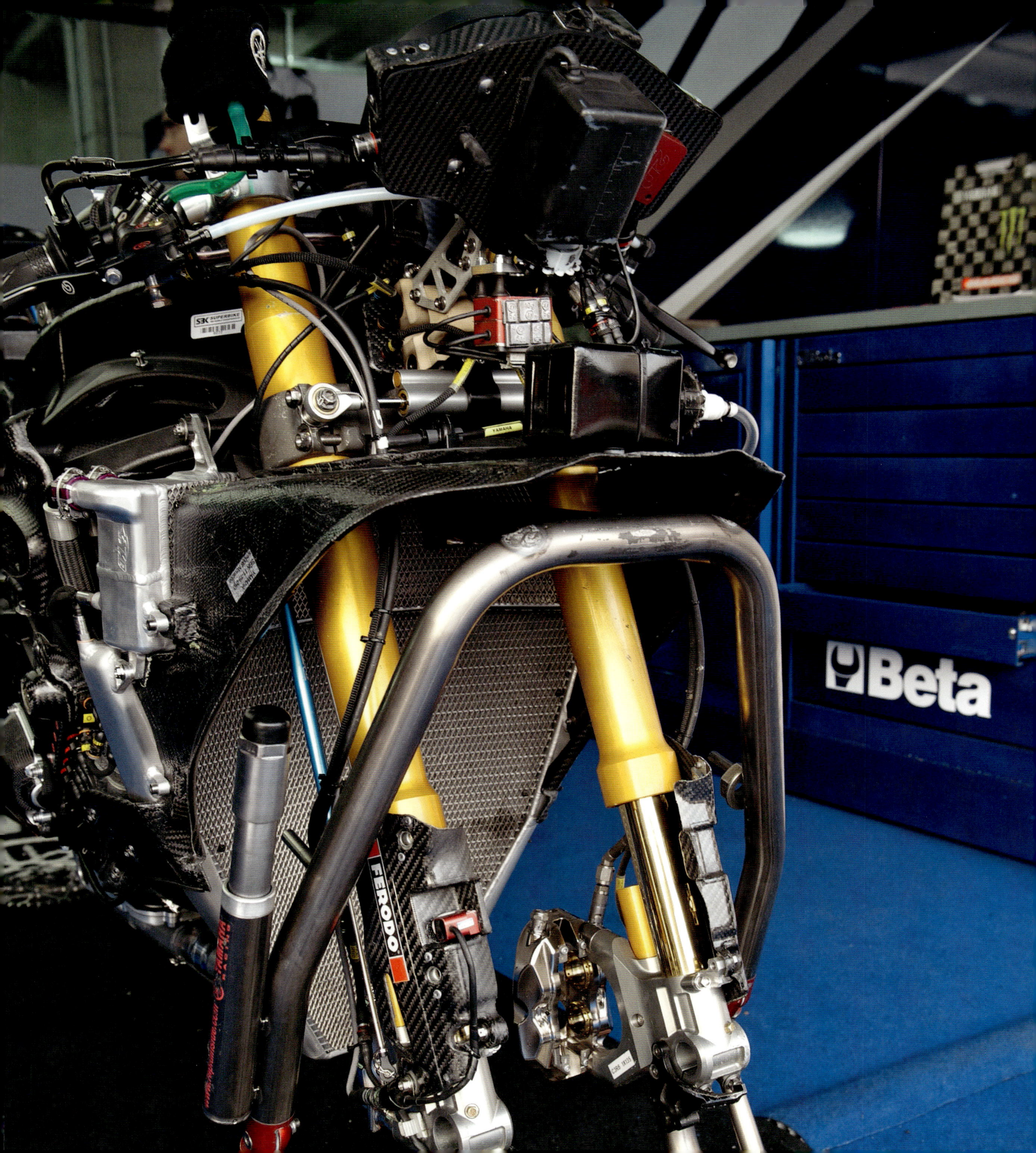
FERODO
Beta

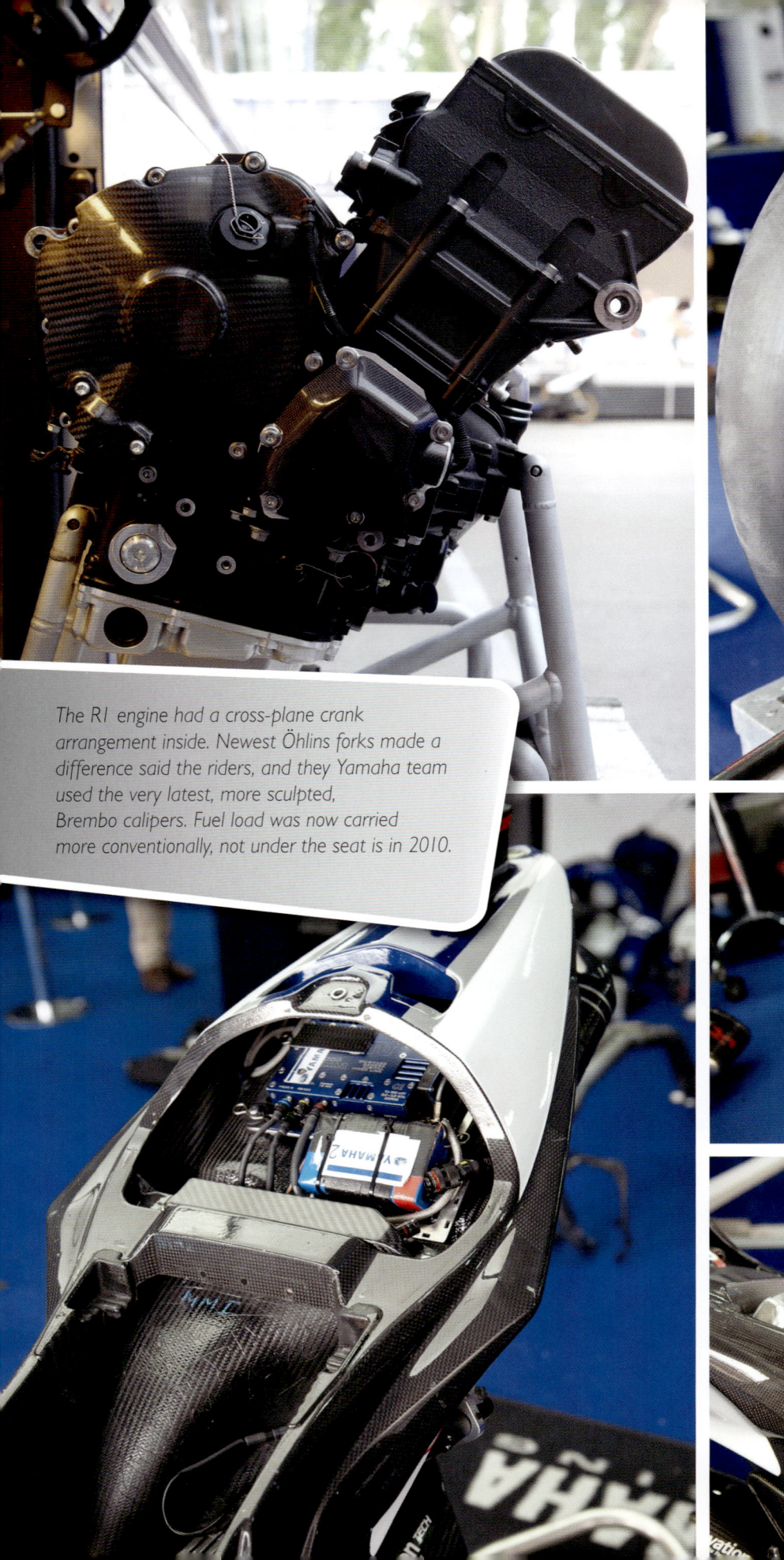

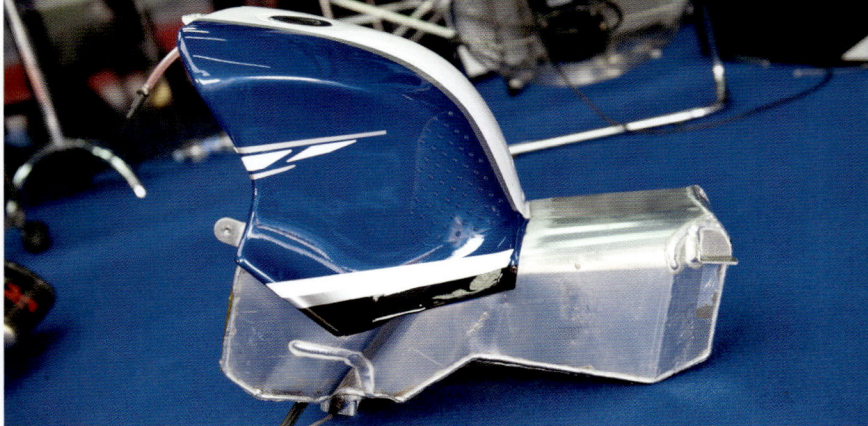

The R1 engine had a cross-plane crank arrangement inside. Newest Öhlins forks made a difference said the riders, and they Yamaha team used the very latest, more sculpted, Brembo calipers. Fuel load was now carried more conventionally, not under the seat is in 2010.

BIKES 2011

to some different sized intake trumpets inside the airbox. The airbox system was the same but featured different lengths on number two and number three cylinders, which make all four-cylinders work the same way. The first prototype of this was made in Italy then Japan sent back the mass produced parts as finished items. Riders felt an improvement in smoothness, important in throttle opening phases.

There were two steps in the engine this year, with 2-3 horsepower found each time.

Yamaha did a good job to get such a rangy bike to work well with featherweight riders Melandri and Laverty, and made so many pure racing developments they had the strongest engine of the year.

TYRES

PIRELLI

Since 2004 Pirelli has been the official one-make tyre supplier for the four classes that make up the Superbike World Championship weekend event programme. The Italian manufacturer has always been present in the production-based racing series but over the past eight seasons its role has taken on primary importance.

The introduction of a single tyre in a championship of such importance was certainly a decision that aroused contrasting reactions at the time but years down the line it turned out to be right choice as well as being extraordinarily valid from a technical point of view.

This success has been achieved thanks to a total commitment from Pirelli, a company that has not only provided riders with increasingly high-performance rubber – as demonstrated by the lap times in the races – but who also wanted their presence in World Superbike to have a major spin-off on the production of road tyres: the slogan "We sell what we race, we race what we sell" has now become a sort of trademark of the brand and demonstrates how experience and technology accumulated in the racing environment are made available for everyday motorcyclists. As a result this helps to explain the vast quantity of development work carried out on racing tyres aimed at improving performance and duration and not just over a one lap sprint.

This latter aspect helps to highlight the level of technology that Pirelli, an International company but one with its racing base in Italy, can express.

Designed in Milan, Italy and produced in Germany, the tyres destined for the Superbike World Championship are managed on-site by a 26-strong staff headed by Pirelli tyre engineer Giorgio Barbier who has been involved in the production-based project almost right from the start.

Around 5,000 tyres are brought to the track at every race and set up in the dedicated Pirelli compound inside the paddock, surrounded by five transport trucks, together with two other vehicles used for the transport of equipment and tools as well as a mobile office truck and hospitality unit.

As mentioned before 26 people comprise the staff present in the circuit, led by Barbier; they also include a Pirelli coordinator, a press officer, six engineers, two track operations managers, a hospitality manager and 14 experienced racing tyre fitters. It's a veritable task force, one that has to satisfy the demands of almost 120 riders by guaranteeing that a range of 28 to 32 different slick, intermediate and rain tyres for the four different classes are instantly available.

The importance of Pirelli's participation in the Superbike World Championship is not only evident from the vast quantity of material available but also from the dedicated compound inside the paddock where the tyres and vehicles are located.

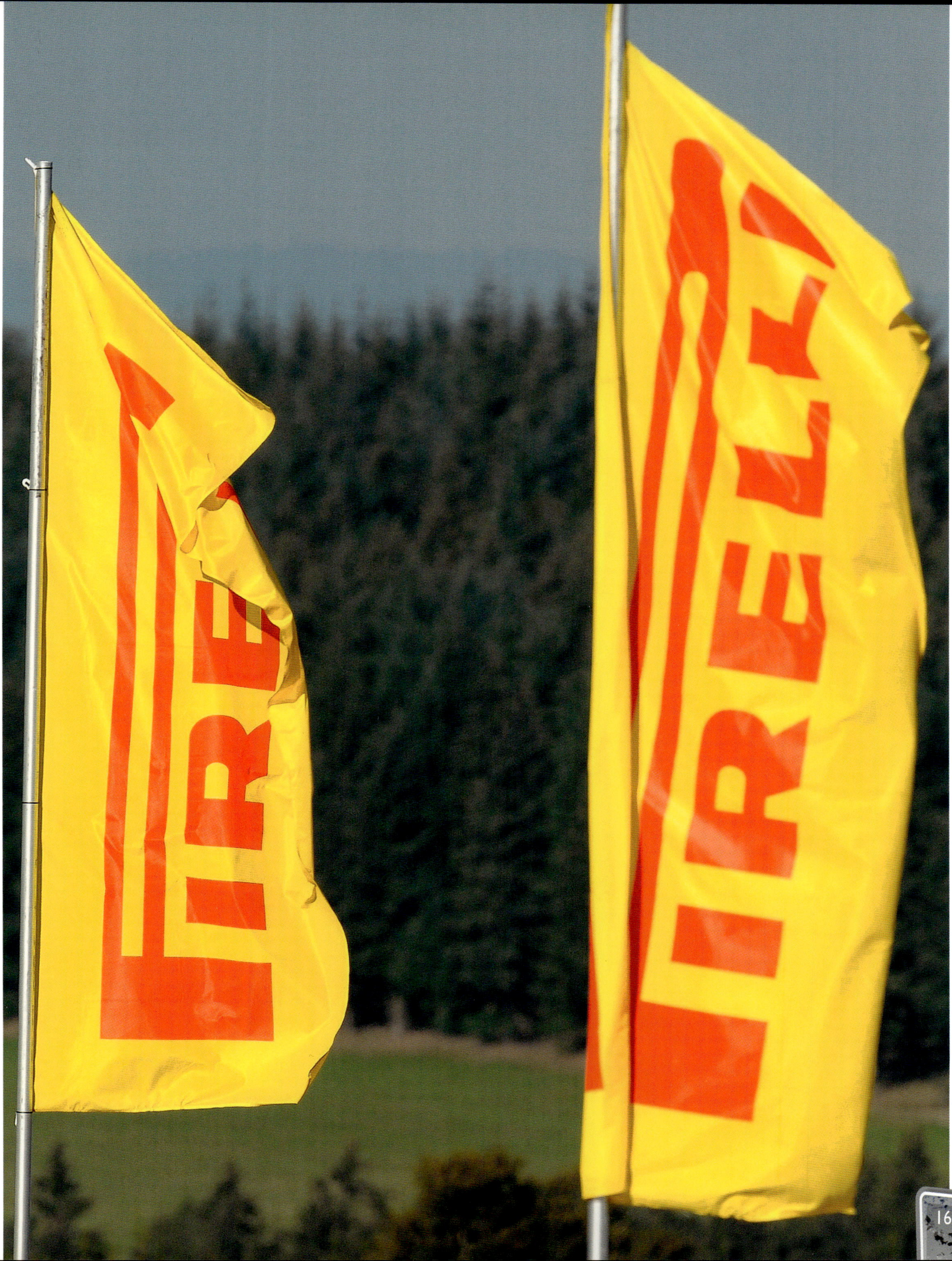

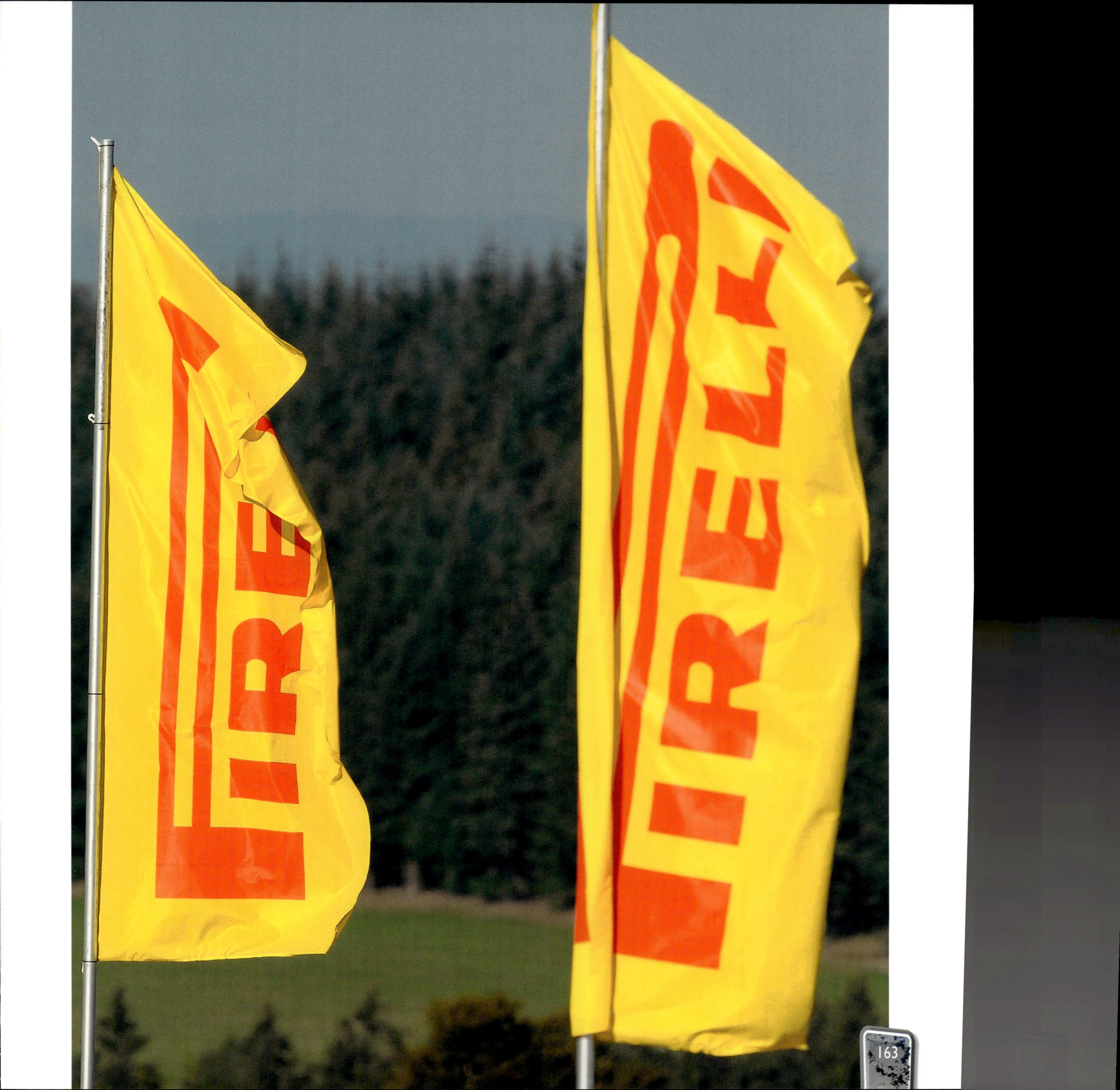

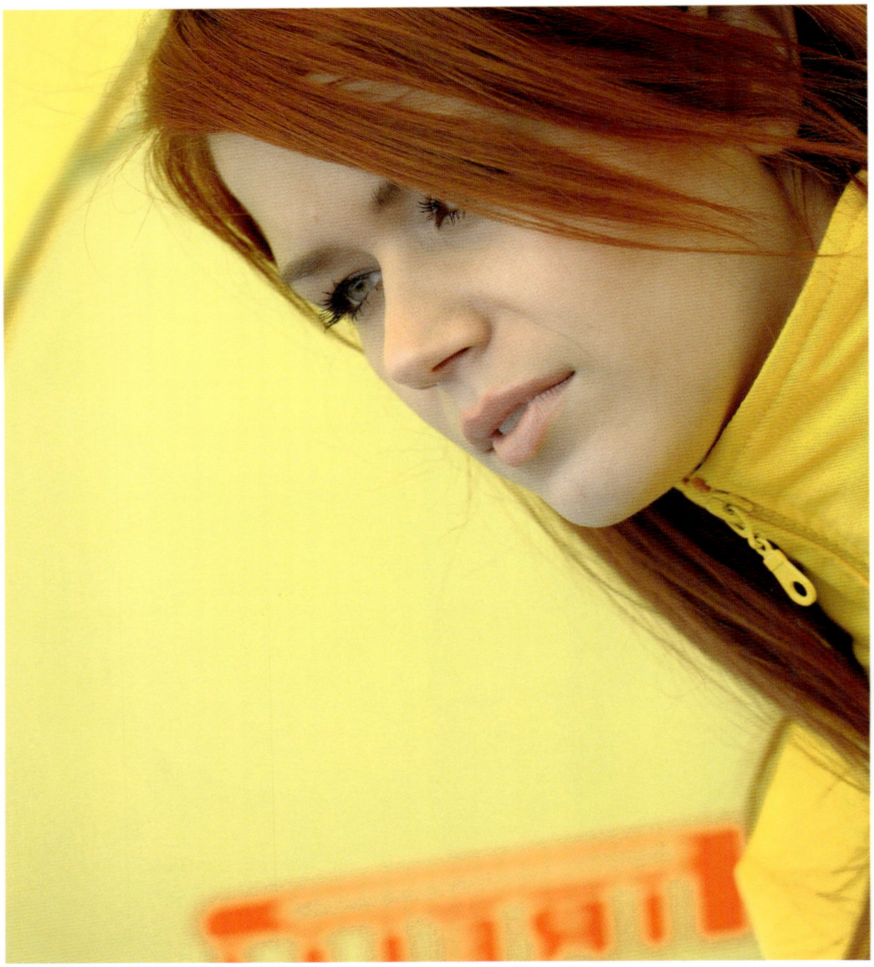

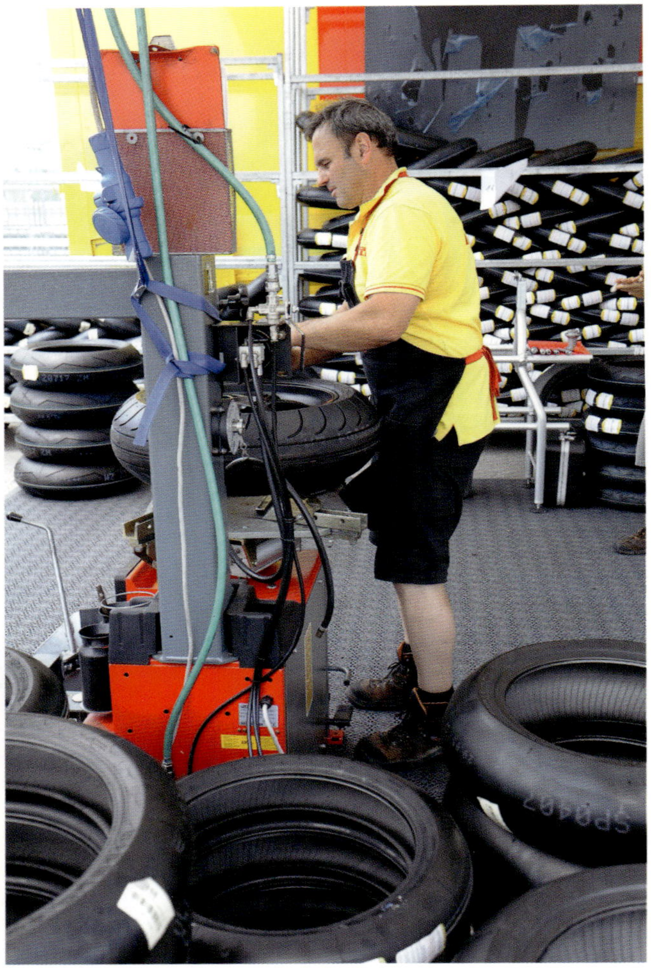

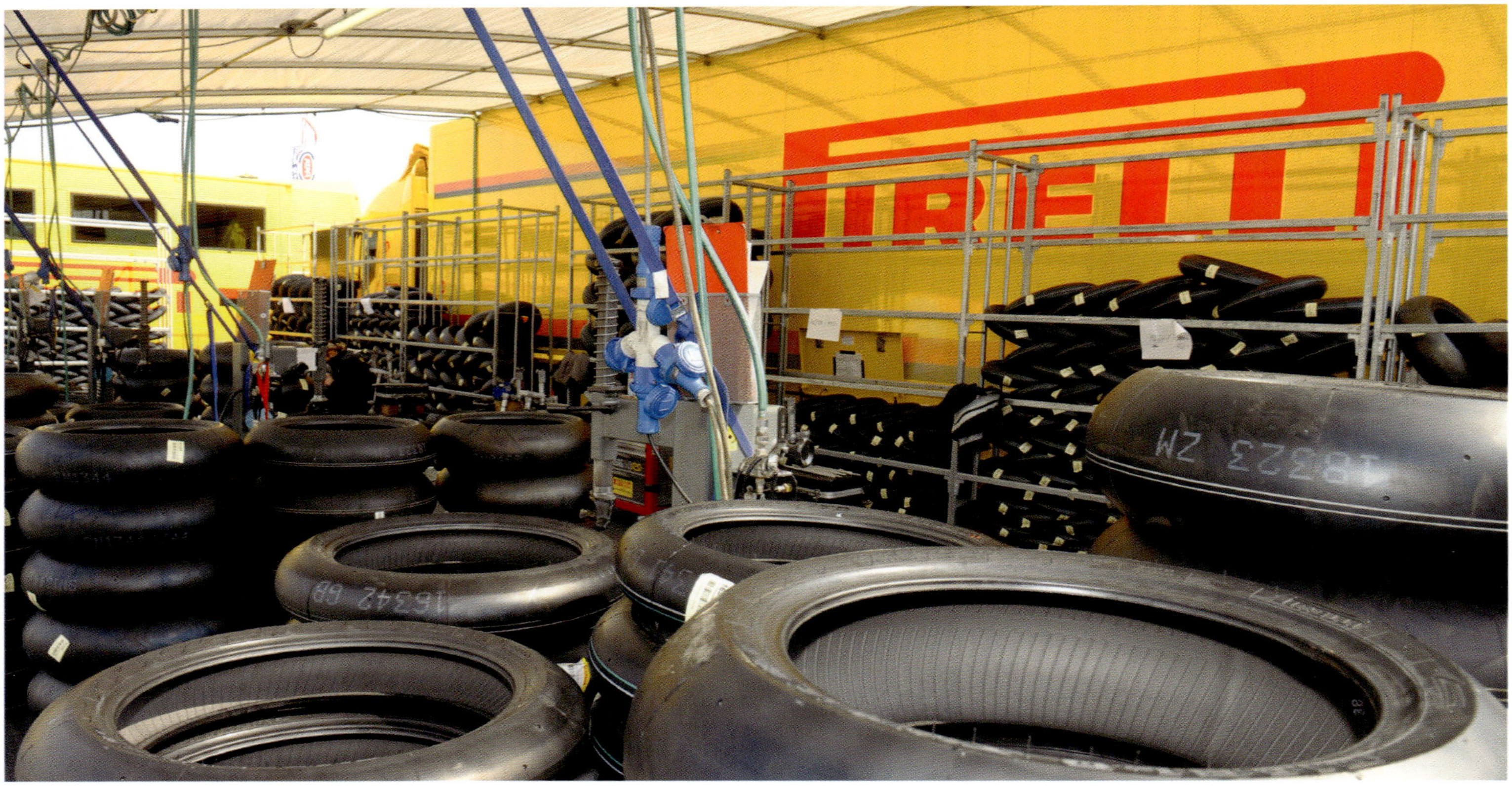

TYRES

Each type of tyre has to be used immediately (and fitted onto the wheel rim), because the time scale is very short in the racing world. As a result space is of the essence, which in Superbike's case means there is an area of around 1,400 square metres for tyre technicians to work in the best possible way. The tyres are fitted under two large awnings, each one containing four assembly lines. Each assembly line is made up of a tyre fitting machine and a balancing machine. In the 'A' tent, assistance is given to riders in the Superbike and Superstock 1000 classes, while the 'B' tent is dedicated to Supersport and Superstock 600. On average, between 2,000 and 2,200 tyres are fitted (and removed) in four days, peaking at 210 tyres per hour!

It is clear that a 360° organization is required, one that is guaranteed by a team of specialized and dedicated personnel. A constant work flow is also guaranteed by special software that allows the situation to be constantly monitored (the correct requests from the teams, the total number of tyres available for the team itself, priority on the basis of the practice and qualifying schedule, reading the bar codes, etc.).

Everything is carried out without neglecting the philosophy that lies at the basis of the Superbike World Championship, that is the contact with the fans who visit the paddock and who have an opportunity not only to 'touch' the racing tyres but also to watch the tyres being fitted and then purchase them from their dealer once they have been put on sale.

Even though it might seem superfluous it is also important not to forget that those vital round black 'things' are the result of lengthy design and development work carried out in Italy by technicians who are often 'on-site' in the circuit to check on how valid their theories are and in order to be able to continue to offer increasingly technologically advanced products.

In short, those round black 'things' are more than just rubber...

After eight years of exclusive supply for the four classes that make up the Superbike World Championship weekend event programme, Pirelli's management of 5,000 tyres per race runs like clockwork.

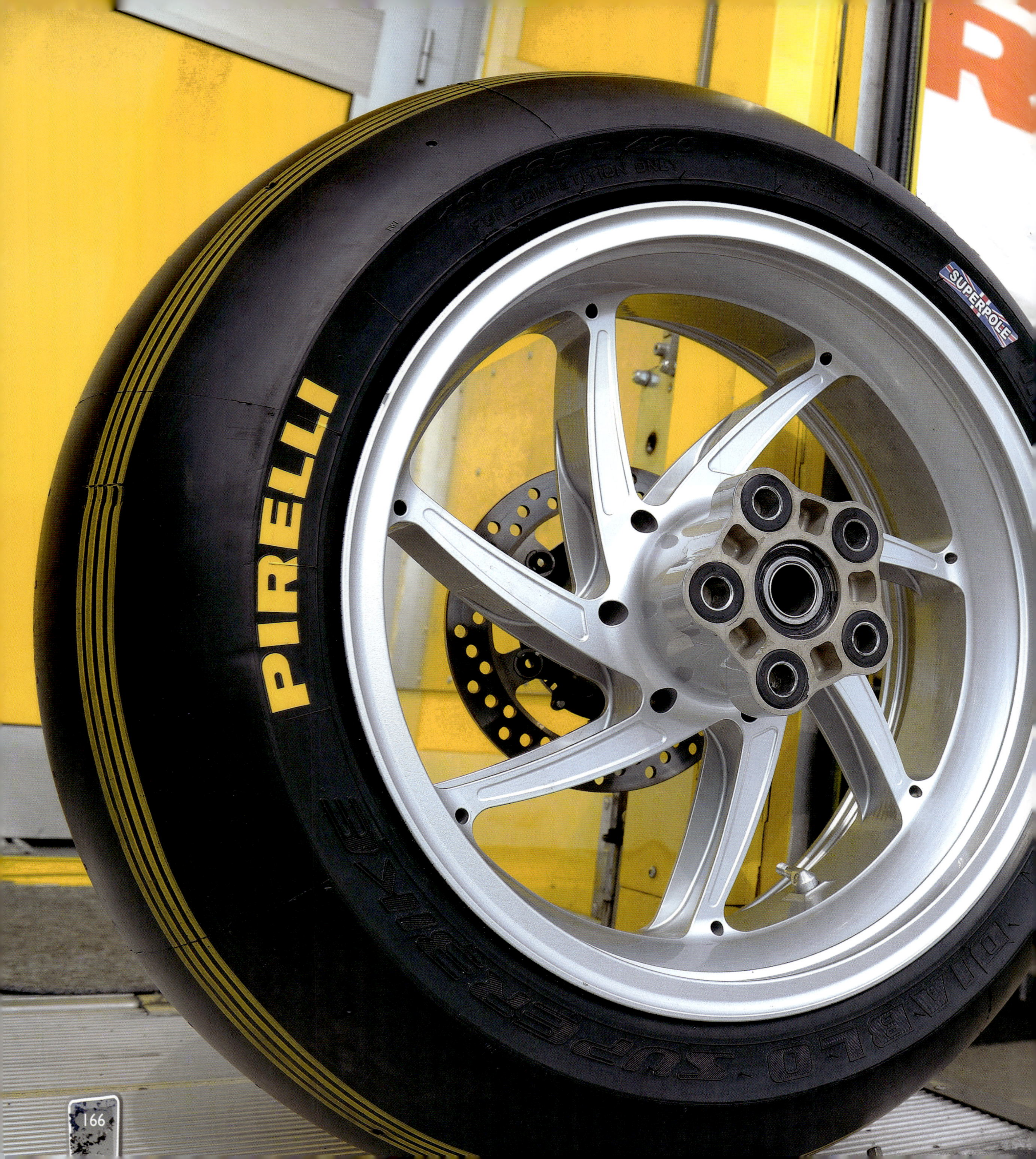
PIRELLI
FOR COMPETITION ONLY
SUPERPOLE
DIABLO SUPERBIKE

One of the aims of Pirelli is to convert the know-how accumulated in World Superbike to the tyres they put on sale for everyday road use. That's one more reason why tyre development is an on-going situation.

WSS CHAMPIONSHIP

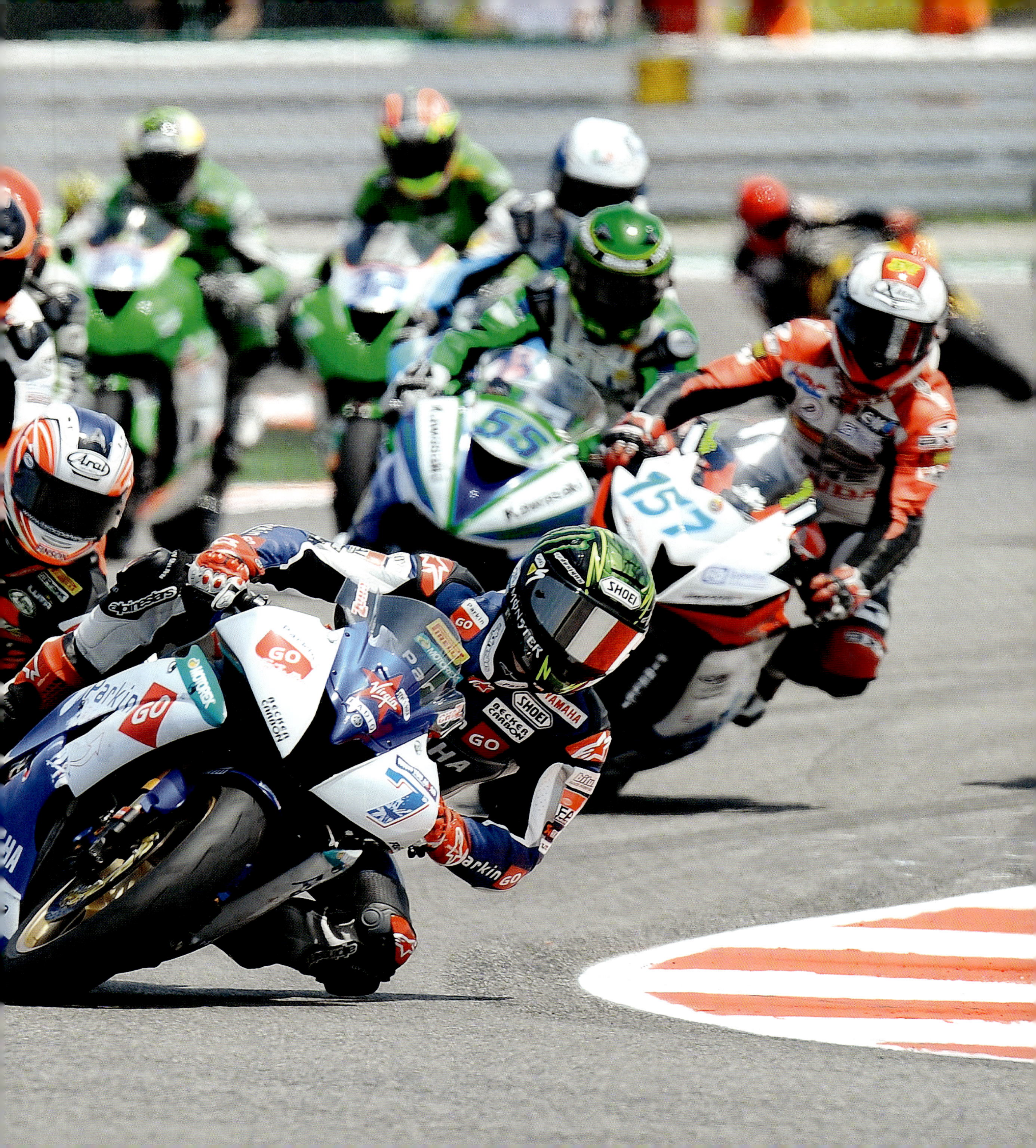
Arai
55
Kawasaki
157
SHOEI
YAMAHA
alpinestars
GO

MAGNY-COURS 2011
SUPERSPORT
CHAZ DAVIES
WORLD SUPERSPORT
CHAMPION 2011
YAMAHA
YAMAHA

WSS CHAMPION

There was no lack of interesting storylines going into the 2011 World Supersport championship. First among them was the possible impact of a rules change which limited each rider to one bike per race weekend, whereas they had always used two in the past. Another open question regarded the performance level of the 2009 WSS championship winning Yamaha R6's, which were returning to action (slightly updated) after a year in storage. The third major storyline concerned the arrival of several promising young riders, who were expected to give the series "veterans" all they could handle.

The use of only one bike per rider turned out to have no ill effects on the racing, and indeed the measure will even be adopted by the Superbike category for 2012, in a continuing effort to save costs.

The former factory Yamaha bikes proved so competitive that they won another world championship, this time with Chaz Davies at the controls, racing for team ParkinGO. The decision by Giuliano Rovelli's team to use the Japanese bikes came at the last minute, and both Davies and his teammate Luca Scassa had actually spent the winter preparing to race their Triumphs from the 2010 season. The British rider had finished fourth that year on the three-cylinder machine, and they were hoping to take another step forward. But after long negotiations with Yamaha Europe, the covers were taken off the R6's that Cal Crutchlow used to such great effect in 2009, and which were retired at the end of that same season. Updated accordingly, the Japanese machines proved to be fast from

The World Supersport title marks the highlight of Chaz Davies' career thus far. The British rider stepped up his game after joining team ParkinGO, with whom he raced on a Triumph last season, and a Yamaha this year.

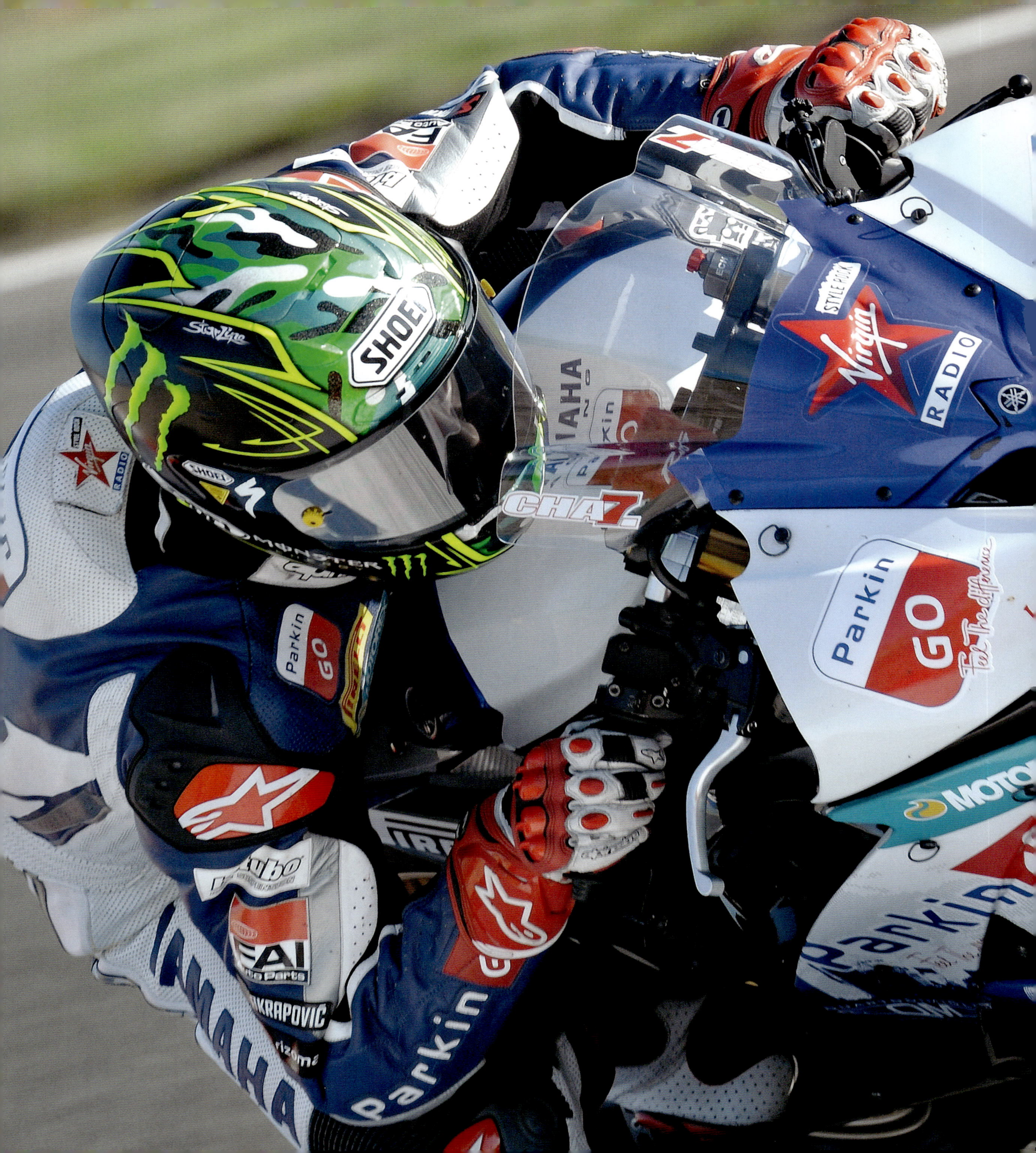

SHOEI
STYLE BOOK
Virgin
RADIO
Parkin
GO
YAMAHA
AKRAPOVIC

Riding the Yamaha R6, a bike that some thought was no longer competitive, Chaz Davies won a total of six races, and Luca Scassa a further two. The British rider will move up to Superbike for 2012.

WSS RIDERS

He didn't manage a race win, but thanks to an extraoridnary level of consistency David Salom (above) finished the year as the runner-up to Davies. It was another season at the front for Fabien Foret (99), riding a Honda for team Ten Kate, the most successful team in the category.

the very start, even allowing Luca Scassa to win the season opening race at Phillip Island. Yamahas would win a further eight races during the season, bringing their 2011 total to nine.

The excitement surrounding the R6 was not just limited to the number of race wins however, as it also extended to those riding the bike in the championship. Scassa managed to win the first two races of the season before crashing out at Assen, but from Monza onward it was Chaz Davies who took control, not only winning at the Italian circuit, but also grabbing the lead in championship points.

This marked the beginning of a series of results which saw the British rider take the world championship, the high point thus far in a career that had been somewhat rocky up until that point. The 24 year old has spent past seasons competing in series as diverse as 250cc GP and the AMA, with mixed results in each. It was a round in the American championship, however, that first brought him into contact with Giuliano Rovelli, who asked him to ride the Triumph in the final few races of 2009. Then, after scoring four podium finishes in 2010, Davies finally found in the Yamaha a bike that would allow him to express his full potential, with the result plain for everyone to see.

Meanwhile his teammate, Luca Scassa – who moved to Supersport after an up and down season in Superbike – can feel satisfied with his fifth place finish in the final standings,

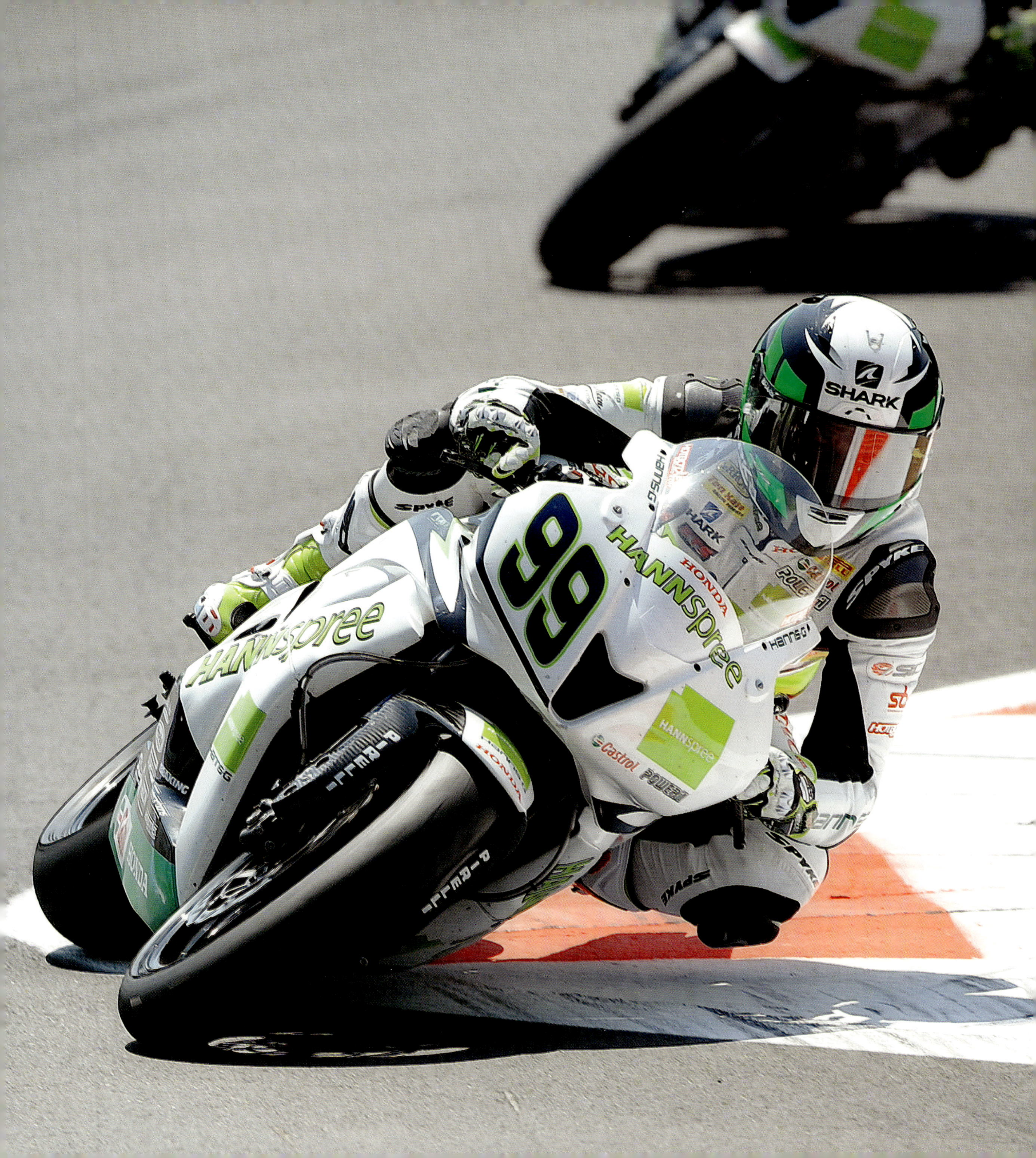
SHARK
99
HANNspree
HONDA
HANNspree
Castrol
SPYKE

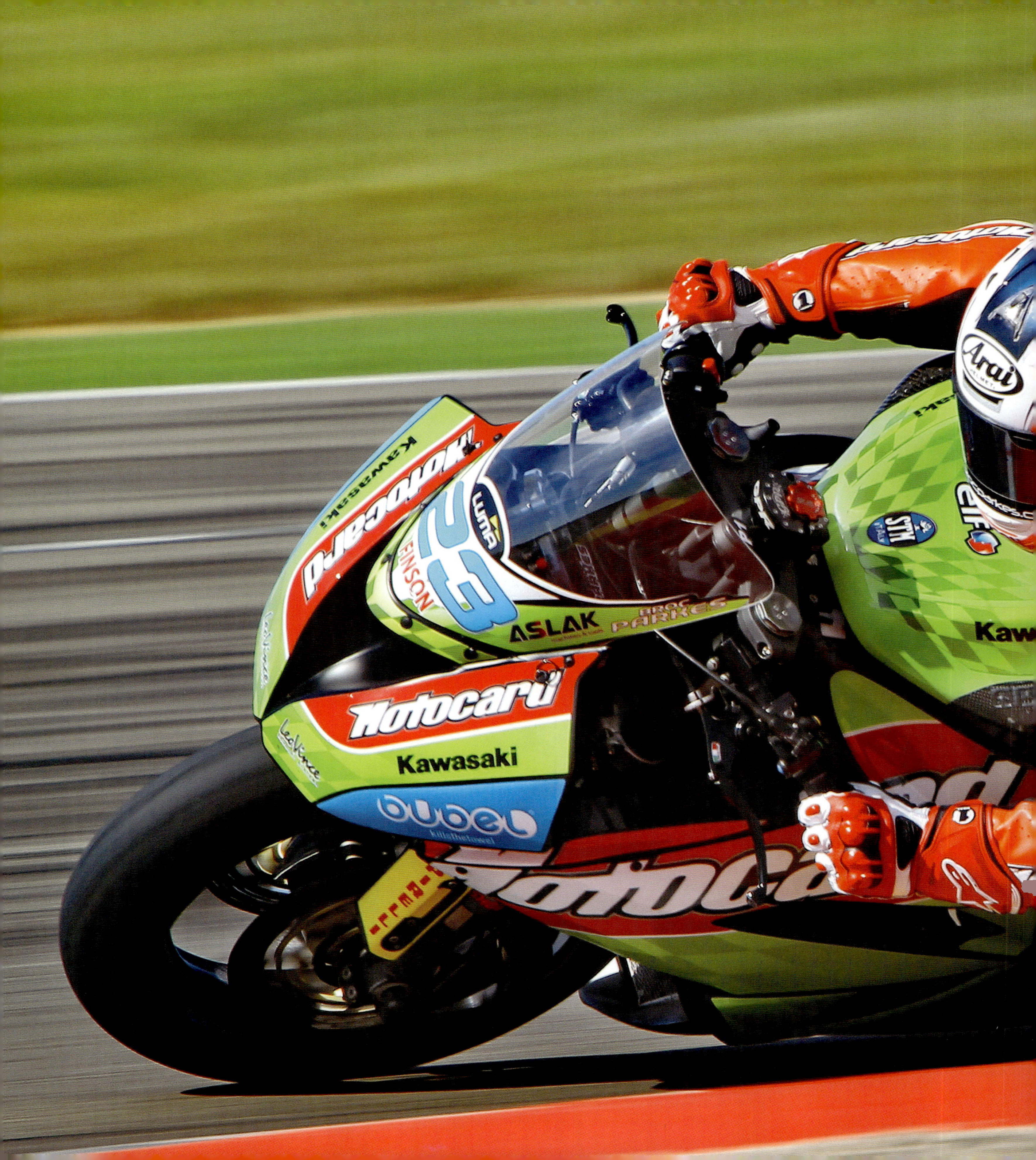
Motocard
Kawasaki
ASLAK
BROC PARKES
Arai

Broc Parkes ran with the front runners all season long on his Kawasaki, scoring a race win at Misano, and finishing the season fourth in points. The Australian returned to Supersport after a stint in Superbike.

178

WSS RIDERS

and the three race wins he registered in the process. The crashes at Assen and Aragon, along with a technical issue at Imola and a disqualification from the Misano round, all took a heavy toll on his final tally.

And while the Yamaha was something of an unknown quantity before the season, the Kawasaki was considered one of the heavy favorites, especially in light of its excellent 2010 performance level. The title of course went to Davies, but riders on the green bikes finished second and fourth in points, notching up six pole positions in the process. The 2011 WSS Championship runner up was therefore David Salom, a 27 year old Spaniard who finished every race of the season, and always in the points. Salom never managed to win a race, but he was on the podium three times (twice in second place).

Managing a win, on the other hand, was his teammate Broc Parkes, a 30 year old Australian making his Supersport return after a spell in Superbike, who was victorious at Misano.

In fact, taking a look at the rider demographics confirms that the "veterans" can still get it done on a 600, starting with Fabien Foret – WSS champion in 2002 – who finished third in this year's championship at the age of 38. The Frenchman won at Imola, and finished on the podium a further five times, all while riding for Honda, the most successful marque in the category.

Surprisingly enough, the Tokyo manufacturer managed only one other win during the season, recorded by the exciting (and frequently crashing) British rider Gino Rea, who triumphed in a wild contest at Brno.

Two British protagonists of the 2011 Supersport Championship: Sam Lowes (11) and James Ellison (77), both riding Hondas. The former race for the Portuguese team Parkalgar, while the latter competed for team Bogdanka PTR.

Luca Scassa started the season in the best of ways, winning both of the first two races, at Phillip Island and Donington Park. After his misstep at Assen and a second place finish at Monza, the Italian rider encountered a series of problems that his Magny Cours win only partially compensated for. Scassa eventually finished the season fifth in championship points.

181

WSS RIDERS

Other featured riders of the 2011 WSS season: Gino Rea (4) winner at Brno, but often in the gravel. Florian Marino (21) finished eighth in his debut season, just ahead of Italian riders Roberto Tamburini (22) and Massimo Roccoli (55), riding for Yamaha and Kawasaki, respectively.

And even if they didn't register any wins, there were other Honda riders making an impact on the championship, such as fellow Britons Sam Lowes (six podium finsihes) and James Ellison, along with 18 year old Frenchman Florian Marino, who made his series debut riding for the same team as Foret.

The Italian contingent – the aforementioned Scassa aside – could have (and should have) accomplished more during the season. This includes Roberto Tamburini and Massimo Roccoli, who got involved in something of a derby (both are from Rimini) as they fought for ninth place in points. In the end it was the former who won out on his Yamaha, getting the best of the latter and his Kawasaki. Both of them recorded a fourth place finish as their best result of the season.

Without any sustained support from the factory, those Triumphs still competing suffered from a drop in competitiveness, despite the best efforts of South African rider Ronan Quarmy and his team Suriano Racing partner Danilo Dell'Omo.

Among the interesting notes for the season was the first ever instance of WSS points being scored by a Russian rider: Vladimir Leonov finished in ninth place at Portimao. It marks an important increase in participation from Eastern European teams and riders (Nemeth, Toth, Ivanov, Szopek, Jezek, ecc), which will culminate in the 2012 World Championship round in Moscow.

183

STK 1000 CHAMPIONSHIP

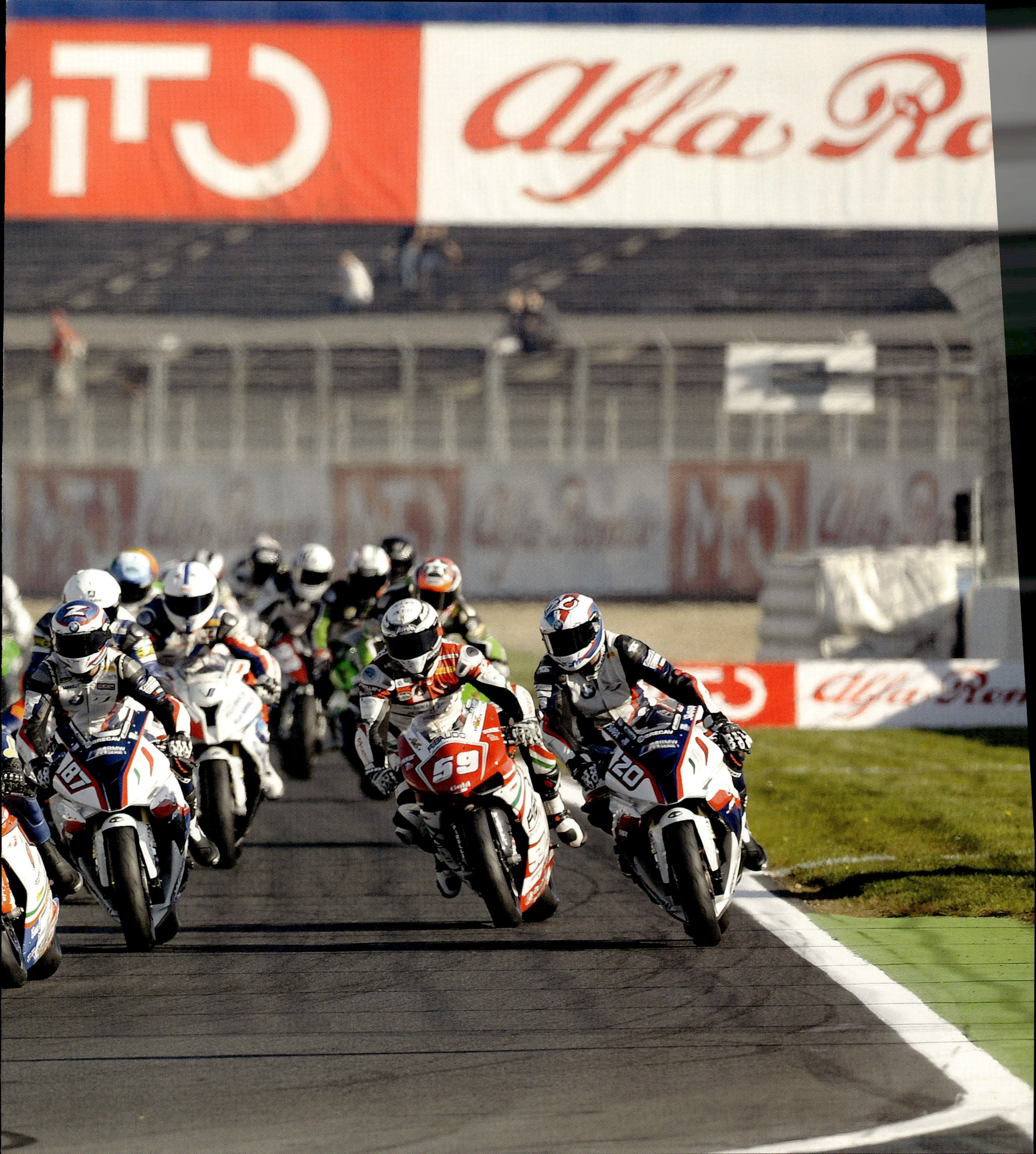
Alfa Ro
187
59
120

186

STK 1000 CHAMPION

As the list of past championship winners clearly demonstrates, the Superstock 1000 category has often seen Italian riders excel. A solid seven of the thirteen title winners (between the European and FIM Cups) have come from Italy. That tradition continued on this season, and not only because Roman rider Davide Giugliano took the title, but also because seven Italian riders finished in the top ten (and eleven in the top fifteen).

Right from the season opening race at Assen (which he won), Davide Giugliano made it clear that he was shooting for the FIM Cup title, continuing to demonstrate his strength at Misano and Aragon. Trying to hold him off were Danilo Petrucci (Ducati) and Lorenzo Zanetti, the latter winning at Monza on a BMW. A victory for Sylvain Barrier (BMW), at Brno, didn't create any problems for Giugliano, whose toughest moment came at Silvertone, when he crashed out of a race that saw Petrucci take the first of his four wins. The Nurburgring saw a return to the top step of the podium for Giugliano, who simply did what was necessary at Imola and Magny Cours to protect his lead and clinch the FIM Cup, one round early. The young Italian (22 years of age) was then rewarded with a one off Ducati WSBK ride at Portimao, where he concluded two satisfying races and showed that his Superstock title was well deserved after all these seasons at the front.

The 2011 season was also dominated by an Italian manufacturer, as Ducati took eight of the twelve race wins. Giugliano and Petrucci took four victories each, but the twin-cylin-

Thanks to the capable support of team Althea, Davide Gugliano (above, with team general manager Genesio Bevilacqua) scored four race wins on the season, the same number recorded by Danilo Petrucci (next to him on the podium).

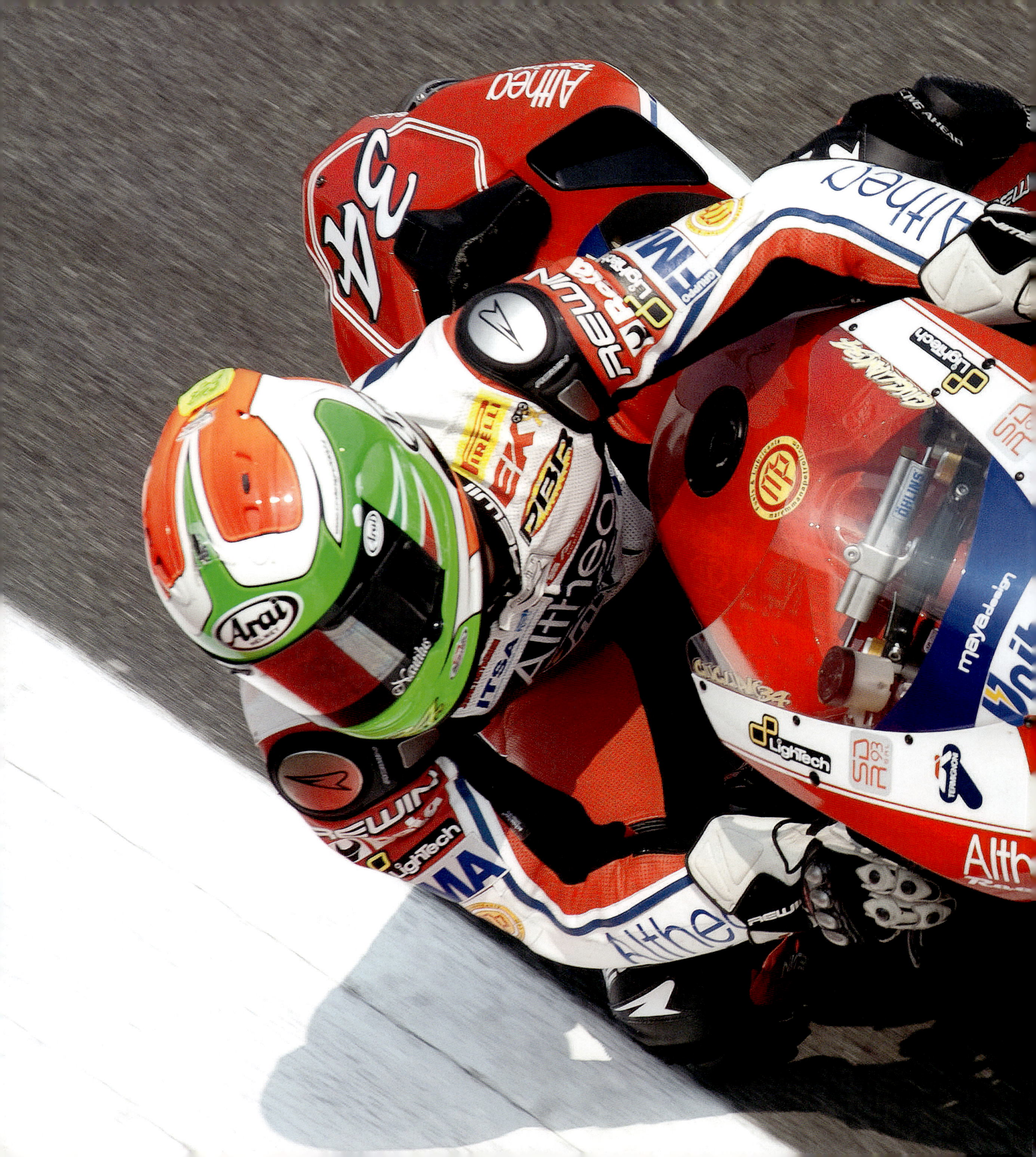

Althea
34
Arai
LighTech
REWIN
mayedesign

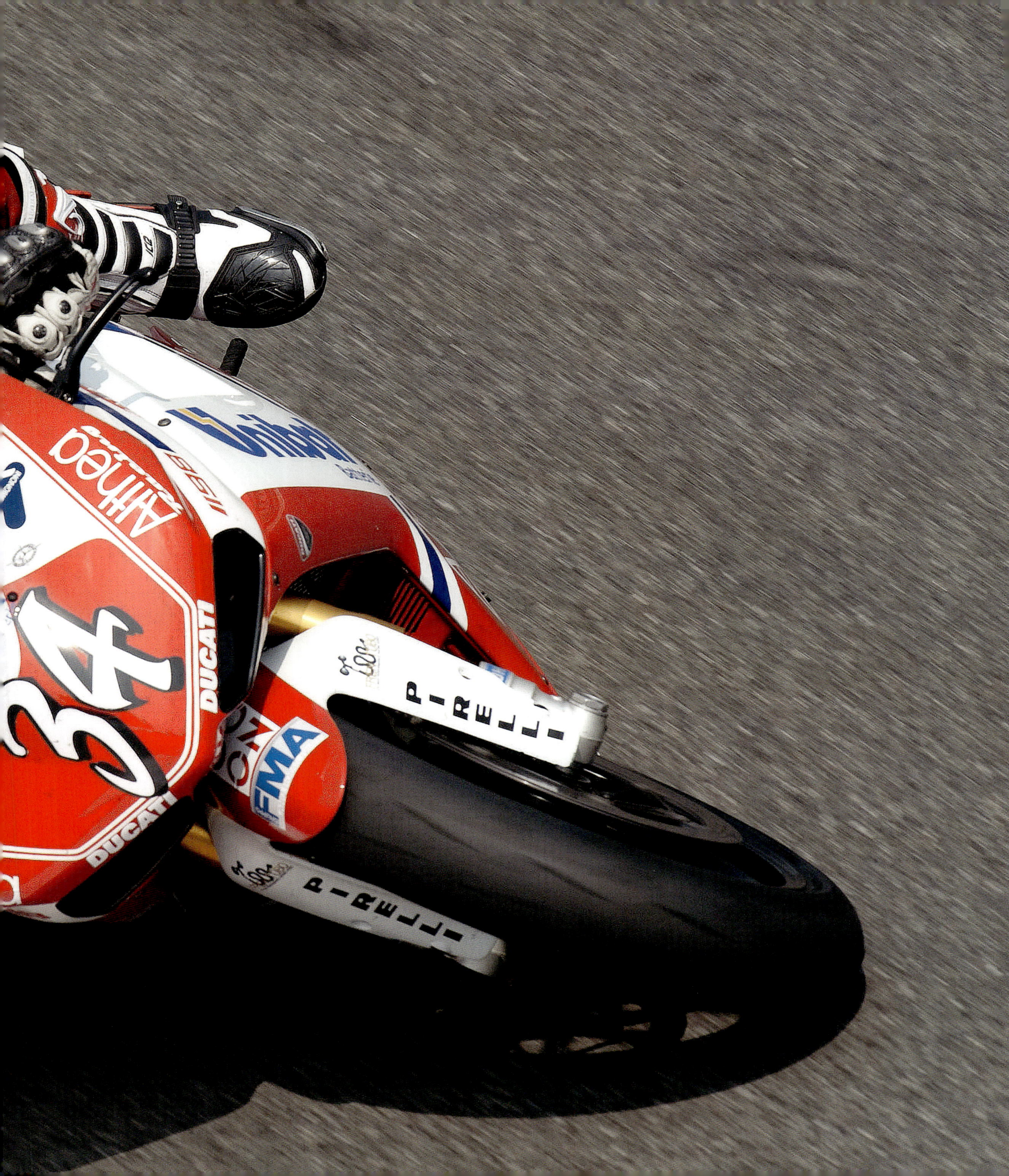
34
DUCATI
DUCATI
FMA
PIRELLI
PIRELLI

STK 1000 RIDERS

After winning the 2010 title with Ayrton Badovini, BMW was once again a force in the series, thanks largely to the performances of Sylvain Barrier and Lorenzo Zanetti. The Italian (87) finsihed third in season points, winning the race at Monza, while the Frenchman, fourth in points, was victorious at Brno.

der machines were constantly near the front of the pack. In fact, beyond the top two finishers in points, we also saw Niccolò Canepa – who won the FIM Cup title in 2007, also on a Ducati – regain his form and score three podium finishes (Silverstone, Nurburgring and Imola). Although he didn't manage a race win, Canepa can look toward 2012 with confidence, as he makes the step up to World Superibke. Also on a Ducati was the fiery Lorenzo Baroni, 21 years old from Ravenna, who partnered with Giugliano at team Althea.

The main competition for the Italian machines came from BMW, the dominant force in the 2010 season (nine out of ten race wins). Leading the charge for the German marque were Lorenzo Zanetti (24 years old from Brescia, Italy) and Sylvain Barrier (23 years old from Oyonnax, France), who each won a single race, allowing them to finish third and fourth in the championship, respectively. Some strong performances on the S 1000 RR also came from young Markus Reiterberger, a very quick 17 year old German ride, who finished eighth in points for his debut international season. Italian Fabio Massei, in his first full season on a 1000cc machine, was ninth in points, while his compatriot Michele Magnoni scored a podium at

87
BMW
Rider Equipement
BMW Motorrad Itali
SPYKE
RR
BMW
SERIE 1
PIRELLI
BOMBOOGIE
PATRIZIO
GEN-ART
ZANETTI

GS car
FERROCART
TERNI
TERNANA
SOCCORSO
TERMIGNONI
DAINESE
PAROFOLI
9
TEAM

Two negative results (Brno and Nurbrurgring) prevented Danilo Petrucci from taking his title fight with Davide Giugliano to the final race. The young Italain nevertheless demonstrated notable levels of talent and composure.

STK 1000 RIDERS

Getting back on a Ducati helped Niccolò Canepa (59) to be competitive once again. Andrea Antonelli (8) did a good job on a slightly less competitive Honda, while Lorenzo Baroni (14) finished seventh in points on a Ducati. The top Kawasaki rider of the season was Sheridan Morais (32).

Monza in one of his few appearances. Although the Honda CBR 1000 RR seemed a little less competitive than its German and Italian counterparts, Andrea Antonelli still managed to finish sixth in overall points, thanks in part to his consistency which saw him scoring points in every round except Misano. The other Japanese mounted riders where much further down in the order.

And speaking of Japanese machinery, there were high expectations for Kawasaki coming into the season, but the green bikes largely failed to deliver on the promise, outside of a few respectable results in the latter stages of the year. The highest placed ZX-10R rider in the season standings was South African Sheridan Morais, who seems to perform well on whatever bike he is riding. The 26 year old from Johannesburg wound up tenth in points, scoring a single podium finish at Portimao. Just behind the team Lorenzini by Leoni rider in the standings we find Bryan Staring, riding the other bike for team Pedercini. The Australian also had more success in the second half of the season than the first, while his teammate Marco Bussolotti almost always finished in the points (Aragon aside).

Practically absent from the grid altogether (with a few race exceptions) was the Yamaha R1, a bike boasting a rich history in Superstock 1000 - James Ellison won the title on it in 2000, Lorenzo Alfonsi in 2004, and Didier van Keymeulen in 2005 – which lately hasn't demonstrated a level of competitiveness on par with its peers.

195

STK 600 CHAMPIONSHIP

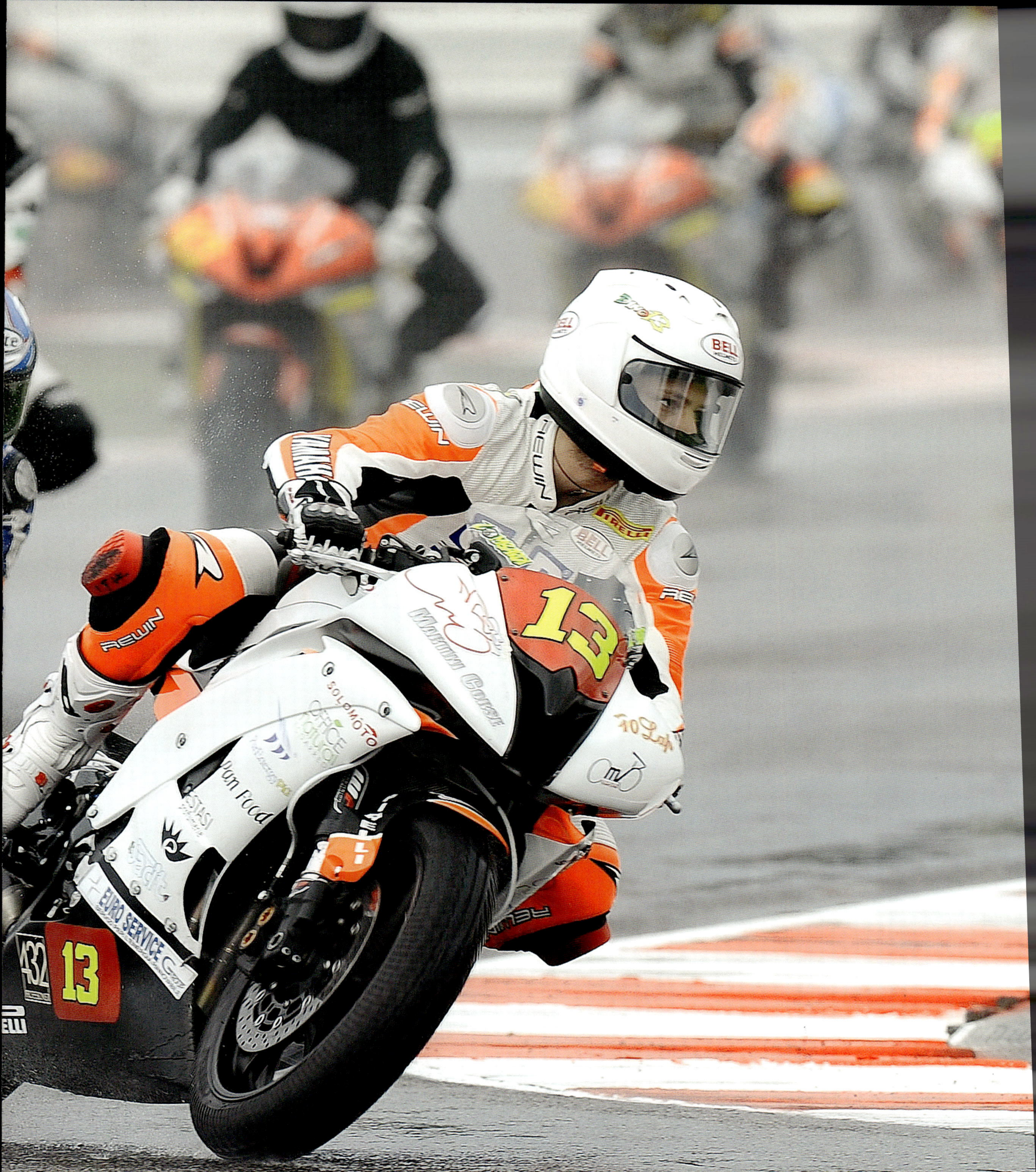
BELL
PIRELLI
REWIN
13
EURO SERVICE
Pan Food
SOLOMOTO
432
13

198

STK 600 CHAMPION

It might seem strange, but the European Superstock 600 championship came down to a contest between two non-European riders: Australian Jed Metcher, and American Joshua Day. Also playing a lead role early in the season was French rider Romain Lanusse, who led the championship up until the Silverstone round. The 16 year old (competing in his second SS600 season) won the race at Monza, and finished on the podium another three times in the first six races of the season. Following that, however, he scored just seven points over the next four rounds, losing the championship lead and sliding all the way back to fourth place.

Italian rider Dino Lombardi, 21 years old and also in his second Superstock 600 season, looked ready to pick up where Lanusse left off (especially after his win at Brno), but he too suffered from a series of setbacks later in the season, eventually finishing the championship in fifth place.

The opening race of the season saw a popular home win for Dutch rider Michael vd Mark at Assen. The team Ten Kate Junior rider, who was making his series debut in that same race, and was using one of the few Hondas on the grid, nullified his additional three wins (Nurburgring, Magny Cours and Portimao) by having some truly poor performances, which all averaged out to third in the championship standings at season's end. He was just one point behind second place.

Authoritatively inserting themselves amongst all these Europeans were the aforementioned Metcher and Day. With a second place finish at Misano, the 15 year old Metcher, riding a Yamaha R6 for team MTM-RT Motorsports, moved up to second place in the champion-

It was Australian Jed Metcher who took home the title in one of the most competitive international motorcycle racing series, Superstock 600, which boasts numerous hungry young riders.

STK 600 RIDERS

Joshua Day (above), was another non-European rider who featured heavily in Superstock 600, riding a bike that wasn't very popular in the series: the Kawasaki. Dutch rider Michael vd Mark (opposite page) scored an impressive four race wins on his Honda.

ship, just behind Lanusse. He further solidified that position with a win at Motorland Aragon. The, following a misstep at Brno, the Australian recorded four consecutive podium finishes, ending the year with a fourth place result at Portimao. This final result – obtained in a conservative performance while keeping an eye on his rival Day – allowed Metcher to seal the Superstock 600 title in his first full season of competition, following an attention grabbing debut race at Magny Cours in 2010.

Joshua Day stayed in with a mathematical shot at the title until the very end, keeping Metcher on his toes and the fans intrigued. The 22 year old American rode a Kawasaki – one of the very few on the grid – for team Revolution Racedays, winning both the Silverstone and Imola rounds. Day competed in three rounds of the 2010 SS600 championship, but this season was his first full time effort, and it produced a rather positive outcome. Despite scoring a podium at Monza, the American didn't get a particularly strong start to his season, but he really picked up momentum following his podium at Brno, a 15th place finish at the Nurburgring (after a crash) the only exception to his later form.

Getting back to the performances of Dino Lombardi, mentioned briefly above, the Italian rider campaigned a Yamaha for team Martini Corse, and there were high hopes for him after he finished third in the 2010 SS600 championship. Initially he looked to be living up to expectations, the strong start to his season

Arai
60
Courageous
MEGA MEGA
Putoline
PIRELLI
EAB
GIBO Groep
MOTOXP

YAMAHA
98

BELL
ARROW
PIRELLI
TEAM TRASIMENO
YAMAHA
Supported Team
TEAM ITALIA
REWIN
YAMAH

RANIERI srl
RIGHINI
MECCANICA SRL
PIRELLI
33

STK 600 RIDERS

highlighted by a win in the Czech Republic, but unfortunately some finishes outside of the top ten (along with the Magny Cours crash) caused him to lose ground quickly in the championship standings. Doing things the other way around was Riccardo Russo, a 19 year old Italian competing for the FMI (Italian Federation) supported Team Italia. He too was on a Yamaha, but his aggressive riding style didn't always translate into promising finishing positions. Once Russo begins to calm down a little bit, he should have no problem managing something more than sixth in the championship.

And speaking of aggressive riders, 21 year old Giuliano Gregorini could certainly have finished further up in the standings, even if he only ran a part time schedule. Riding a Yamaha for team RCGM, the Italian won the Misano race, but didn't do much else in his other appearances.

Scoring two podium finishes was Belgian rider Gauthier Duwelz (teammate to Metcher), who finsihed the year sixth in points, just ahead of Dutchman Tony Covena, French rider Stéphane Egea, and Italians Francesco Cocco (just 15 years old) and Daniele Beretta.

It was interesting to note the large number of Yamaha R6's used in the series, as the Japanese manufacturer monopolized most of the top finishing positions. The few exceptions included the Kawasaki of Josh Day, the Honda of vd Mark, and the Triumph Daytona 675 of Riccardo Cecchini. The R6's ease of use was certainly one of the factors which contributed to its popularity, but the performances of Day and vd Mark will probably help to diversify next year's Superstock 600 grid.

French rider Romain Lanusse (98) started off the year very strongly. Also taking race wins in 2011 were Dino Lombardi (13), the highest finishing Italian, and Giuliano Gregorini (33), while Riccardo Russo (below at left) had a solid season overall.

STANDINGS

SUPERBIKE

1°	C. Checa	(ESP - Ducati)	505 p.
2°	M. Melandri	(ITA - Yamaha)	395
3°	M. Biaggi	(ITA - Aprilia)	303
4°	E. Laverty	(IRL - Yamaha)	303
5°	L. Haslam	(GBR - BMW)	224
6°	S. Guintoli	(FRA - Ducati)	210
7°	L. Camier	(GBR - Aprilia)	208
8°	N. Haga	(JPN - Aprilia)	176
9°	J. Rea	(GBR - Honda)	170
10°	A. Badovini	(ITA - BMW)	165
11°	J. Lascorz	(ESP - Kawasaki)	161
12°	M. Fabrizio	(ITA - Suzuki)	152
13°	T. Sykes	(GBR - Kawasaki)	141
14°	J. Smrz	(CZECH - Ducati)	127
15°	T. Corser	(AUS - BMW)	87
16°	M. Berger	(FRA - Ducati)	64
17°	R. Xaus	(ESP - Honda)	49
18°	R. Rolfo	(ITA - Kawasaki)	42
19°	M. Aitchison	(AUS - Kawasaki)	36
20°	J. Hopkins	(USA - Suzuki)	20
21°	C. Vermeulen	(AUS - Kawasaki)	14
22°	J. Toseland	(GBR - BMW)	13
23°	J. Fores	(ESP - BMW)	12
24°	L. Lanzi	(ITA - BMW)	10
25°	J. Waters	(AUS - Suzuki)	8
26°	F. Sandi	(ITA - Ducati)	7
27°	A. Polita	(ITA - Ducati)	5
28°	D. Giugliano	(ITA - Ducati)	4
29°	M. Baiocco	(ITA - Ducati)	4
30°	B. Veneman	(NED - BMW)	3
31°	J. Kirkham	(GBR - Suzuki)	3
32°	V. Kispataki	(H - Honda)	1
33°	A. Lowes	(GBR - Honda)	1
34°	F. Lai	(ITA - Honda)	1
35°	B. Staring	(GBR - Kawasaki)	1

SUPERSPORT

1°	C. Davies	(GBR - Yamaha)	206 p.
2°	D. Salom	(ESP - Kawasaki)	156
3°	F. Foret	(FRA - Honda)	148
4°	B. Parkes	(AUS - Kawasaki)	136
5°	L. Scassa	(ITA - Yamaha)	134
6°	S. Lowes	(GBR - Honda)	129
7°	J. Ellison	(GBR - Honda)	99
8°	F. Marino	(FRA - Honda)	89
9°	R. Tamburini	(ITA - Yamaha)	80
10°	M. Roccoli	(ITA - Kawasaki)	71
11°	G. Rea	(GBR - Honda)	69
12°	R. Harms	(DNK - Honda)	59
13°	M. Praia	(POR - Honda)	51
14°	V. Iannuzzo	(ITA - Kawasaki)	44
15°	B. Nemeth	(H - Honda)	42
16°	A. Lundh	(SWE - Honda)	29
17°	D. Dell'Omo	(ITA - Triumph)	26
18°	R. Quarmby	(RSA - Triumph)	14
19°	I. Toth	(H - Honda)	13
20°	V. Ivanov	(RUS - Honda)	12
21°	P. Szkopek	(PL - Honda)	12
22°	I. Dionisi	(ITA - Honda)	11
23°	O. Jezek	(CZECH - Honda)	9
24°	V. Leonov	(RU - Yamaha)	7
25°	S. Cruciani	(ITA - Kawasaki)	7
26°	B. Chesaux	(CH - Honda)	6
27°	M. Giansanti	(ITA - Kawasaki)	4
28°	M. Jerman	(SK - Triumph)	4
29°	P. Vostárek	(CZECH - Honda)	3
30°	A. Velini	(ITA - Honda)	3
31°	L. Marconi	(GBR - Suzuki)	3
32°	R. Stamm	(H - Honda)	2
33°	L. Bulle	(F - Yamaha)	1
34°	R. Muresan	(MD - Honda)	1

SUPERSTOCK 1000

1°	D. Giugliano	(ITA - Ducati)	171 p.
2°	D. Petrucci	(ITA - Ducati)	169
3°	L. Zanetti	(ITA - BMW)	148
4°	S. Barrier	(FRA - BMW)	132
5°	N. Canepa	(ITA - Ducati)	109
6°	A. Antonelli	(ITA - Honda)	77
7°	L. Baroni	(ITA - Ducati)	74
8°	M. Reiterberger	(GER - BMW)	69
9°	F. Massei	(ITA - BMW)	69
10°	S. Morais	(RSA - Kawasaki)	65
11°	B. Staring	(AUS - Kawasaki)	56
12°	M. Bussolotti	(ITA - Kawasaki)	50
13°	M. Magnoni	(ITA - BMW)	34
14°	E. La Marra	(ITA - Honda)	32
15°	L. Savadori	(ITA - Kawasaki)	31
16°	L. Mercado	(ARG - Kawasaki)	20
17°	J. Guarnoni	(FRA - Yamaha)	16
18°	L. Verdini	(ITA - Kawasaki)	11
19°	L. Baz	(FRA - Honda)	9
20°	B. McCormick	(CAN - BMW)	9
21°	R. Ten Napel	(NED - Honda)	8
22°	T. Svitok	(SVK - Ducati)	8
23°	M. Lussiana	(FRA - BMW)	7
24°	F. Lamborghini	(ITA - Honda)	7
25°	M. Savary	(CH - BMW)	4
26°	R. Fusco	(ITA - BMW)	4
27°	B. Beaton	(AUS - BMW)	3
28°	C. Bergman	(SWE - Kawasaki)	2
29°	D. Buchan	(GBR - Kawasaki)	2
30°	D. Beretta	(ITA - Honda)	2
31°	D. Rivas	(ESP - Kawasaki)	1
32°	R. Pagaud	(FRA - BMW)	1

SUPERSTOCK 600

1°	J. Metcher	(AUS - Yamaha)	150 p.
2°	J. Day	(USA - KAwasaki)	138
3°	M. Vd Mark	(NED - Honda)	137
4°	R. Lanusse	(FRA - Yamaha)	101
5°	D. Lombardi	(ITA - Yamaha)	96
6°	R. Russo	(ITA - Yamaha)	94
7°	G. Duwelz	(BEL - Yamaha)	67
8°	T. Covena	(NED - Yamaha)	50
9°	S. Egea	(FRA - Yamaha)	44
10°	F. Cocco	(ITA - Yamaha)	39
11°	D. Beretta	(ITA - Yamaha)	38
12°	T. Krajci	(SVK - Yamaha)	37
13°	G. Gregorini	(ITA - Yamaha)	35
14°	A. Schacht	(DEN - Honda)	35
15°	N. Calero Perez	(ESP - Yamaha)	35
16°	A. Nestorovic	(AUS - Yamaha)	34
17°	F. Morbidelli	(ITA - Yamaha)	32
18°	J. Elliott	(GBR - Yamaha)	32
19°	N. Morrentino	(ITA - Yamaha)	26
20°	R. Cecchini	(ITA - Triumph)	20
21°	M. Vrajitoru	(ROU - Yamaha)	20
22°	L. Vitali	(ITA - Yamaha)	17
23°	N. Major	(FRA - Yamaha)	16
24°	F. Dittadi	(ITA - Yamaha)	13
25°	C. Gamarino	(ITA - Kawasaki)	12
26°	R. Mulhauser	(CH - Yamaha)	11
27°	M. Marchal	(FRA - Yamaha)	10
28°	J. Pascarella	(USA - Honda)	10
29°	C. Ponsson	(LUX - Yamaha)	10
30°	F. Monti	(ITA - Yamaha)	8
31°	G. Di Carlo	(FRA - Yamaha)	7
32°	R. De Tournay	(FRA - Yamaha)	5
33°	S. Suchet	(CH - Honda)	4
34°	C. Chevrier	(FRA - Triumph)	4
35°	G. Romano	(ITA - Yamaha)	4
36°	A. DeHaven	(USA - Yamaha)	4
37°	J. Wainwright	(GBR - Suzuki)	2
38°	T. Lentink	(NED - Honda)	2
39°	K. Szalai	(FRA - Yamaha)	1

WORLD SUPERBIKE

1988	F. MERKEL	USA	HONDA
1989	F. MERKEL	USA	HONDA
1990	R. ROCHE	F	DUCATI
1991	D. POLEN	USA	DUCATI
1992	D. POLEN	USA	DUCATI
1993	S. RUSSELL	USA	KAWASAKI
1994	C. FOGARTY	GBR	DUCATI
1995	C. FOGARTY	GBR	DUCATI
1996	T. CORSER	AUS	DUCATI
1997	J. KOCINSKI	USA	HONDA
1998	C. FOGARTY	GBR	DUCATI
1999	C. FOGARTY	GBR	DUCATI
2000	C. EDWARDS	USA	HONDA
2001	T. BAYLISS	AUS	DUCATI
2002	C. EDWARDS	USA	HONDA
2003	N. HODGSON	GBR	DUCATI
2004	J. TOSELAND	GBR	DUCATI
2005	T. CORSER	AUS	SUZUKI
2006	T. BAYLISS	AUS	DUCATI
2007	J. TOSELAND	GBR	HONDA
2008	T. BAYLISS	AUS	DUCATI
2009	B. SPIES	USA	YAMAHA
2010	M. BIAGGI	ITA	APRILIA
2011	C. CHECA	ESP	DUCATI

SUPERSPORT WORLD SERIES

1997	P. CASOLI	ITA	DUCATI
1998	F. PIROVANO	ITA	SUZUKI

WORLD SUPERSPORT

1999	S. CHAMBON	FRA	SUZUKI
2000	J. TEUCHERT	GER	YAMAHA
2001	A. PITT	AUS	KAWASAKI
2002	F. FORET	FRA	HONDA
2003	C. VERMEULEN	AUS	HONDA
2004	K. MUGGERIDGE	AUS	HONDA
2005	S. CHARPENTIER	FRA	HONDA
2006	S. CHARPENTIER	FRA	HONDA
2007	K. SOFUOGLU	TUR	HONDA
2008	A. PITT	AUS	HONDA
2009	C. CRUTCHLOW	GBR	YAMAHA
2010	K. SOFUOGLU	TUR	HONDA
2011	D. DAVIES	GBR	YAMAHA

EUROPEAN SUPERSTOCK 1000

2000	J. ELLISON	GBR	YAMAHA
2001	J. ELLISON	GBR	SUZUKI
2002	V. IANNUZZO	ITA	SUZUKI
2003	M. FABRIZIO	ITA	SUZUKI
2004	L. ALFONSI	ITA	YAMAHA

FIM SUPERSTOCK 1000

2005	D. VAN KEYMEULEN	BEL	YAMAHA
2006	A. POLITA	ITA	SUZUKI
2007	N. CANEPA	ITA	DUCATI
2008	B. ROBERTS	AUS	DUCATI
2009	X. SIMEON	BEL	DUCATI
2010	A. BADOVINI	ITA	BMW
2011	D. GIUGLIANO	ITA	DU CATI

EUROPEAN SUPERSTOCK 600

2005	C. CORTI	ITA	YAMAHA
2006	X. SIMEON	BEL	SUZUKI
2007	M. BERGER	FRA	YAMAHA
2008	L. BAZ	FRA	YAMAHA
2009	G. REA	GBR	HONDA
2010	J. GUARNONI	FRA	YAMAHA
2011	J. METCHER	AUS	YAMAHA

CHAMPIONS

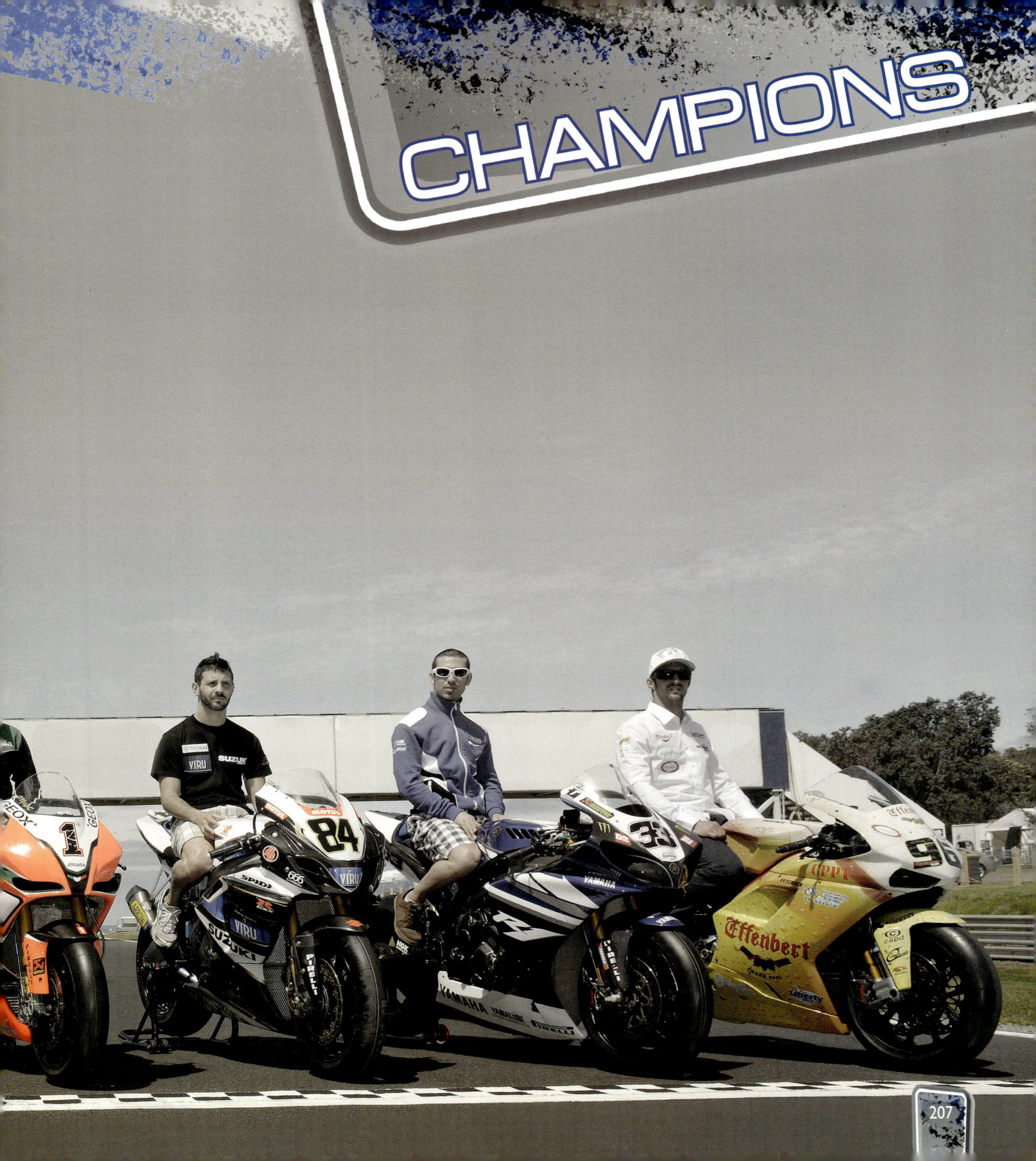

Printed by
Grafiche Flaminia - Foligno (PG)
November 2011

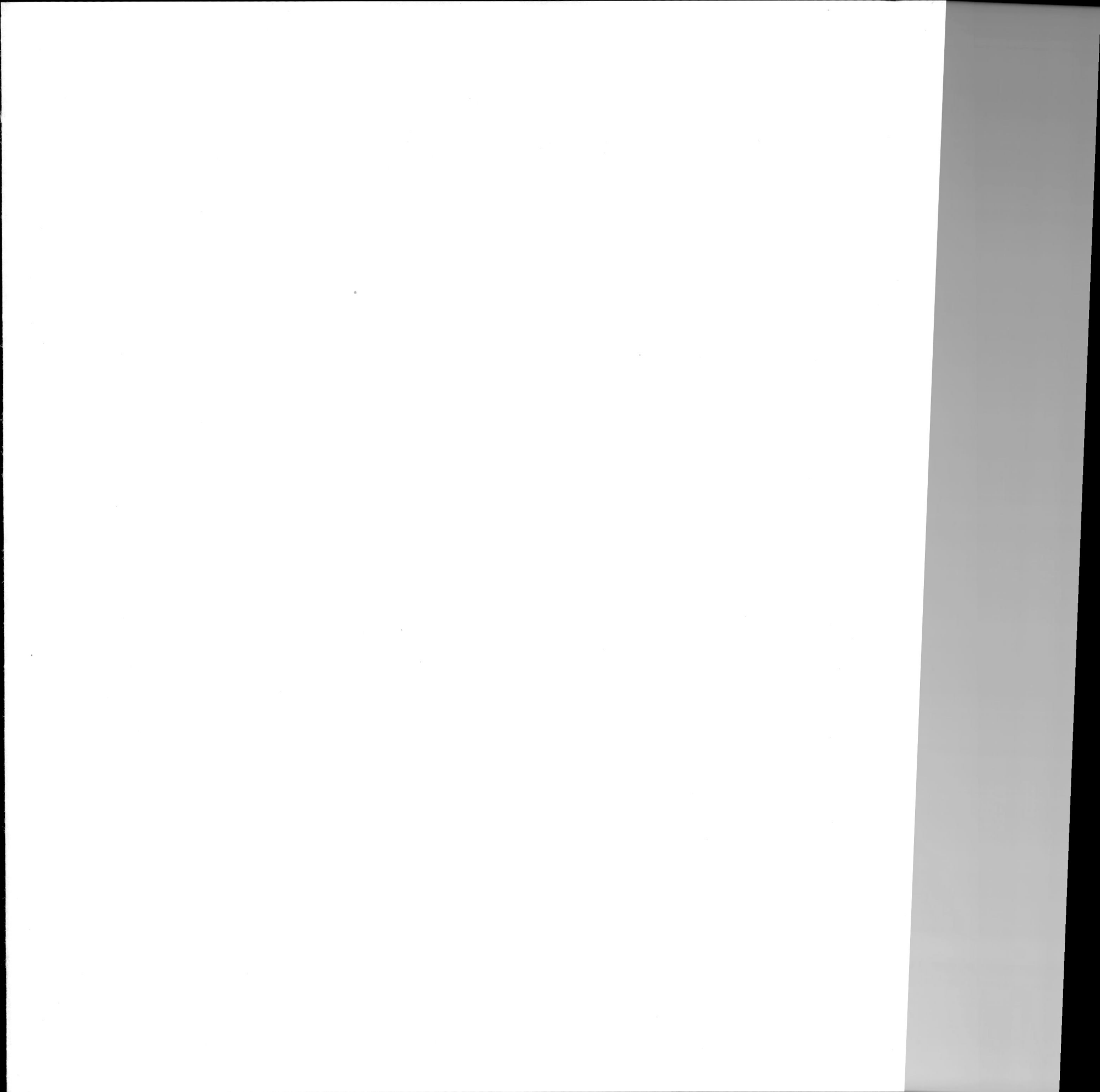